ANGLO-SAXON
JEWELLERY

RONALD JESSUP

ANGLO-SAXON JEWELLERY

SHIRE ARCHAEOLOGY

Published by
SHIRE PUBLICATIONS LTD.
Cromwell House, Church Street, Princes Risborough,
Aylesbury, Buckinghamshire, U.K.

Series Editor: James Dyer

ISBN 0 85263 261 4 (casebound)
ISBN 0 85263 262 2 (paperback)

First published 1974

PRINTED AND BOUND IN GREAT BRITAIN BY
MAUND & IRVINE LTD., TRING

Contents

The author and publishers acknowledge with gratitude the following for provision of and permission to reproduce the photographs indicated:

The Trustees of the British Museum: **1**.1-8; **2**; **5**.9, 11; **7**; **8**; **9**; **14**; **16**.1-2; **17**; **24**.1-3, 8; **25**.1; **27**; **28**; **29**; **30**; **31**.

Department of Antiquities, Ashmolean Museum, Oxford: **3**.1; **5**.10; **15**; **18**; **19**; **23**.3-5; **24**.10; **32**; **33**.

Cambridge University Museum of Archaeology and Ethnology: **6**.2; **12**; **13**; **22**.

Victoria and Albert Museum. Crown Copyright: **24**.5-7, 9.

Copyright: Institute of Archaeology, Oxford: **26**.

The Dean and Chapter of Durham: **4**.

The Royal Museum, Canterbury: **3**.2.

Kent Archaeological Society's Collection, Maidstone: **5**.1-8; **6**.1; **23**.1; **25**.2.

Leicester City Museums and Art Gallery: **10**; **11**.

City of Liverpool Museums: **20**.

Gravesend Public Library: **23**.2.

Victoria and Albert Museum, Waterton Collection: **24**.4.

1
Introduction

Jewellery is both a mirror of life and a footnote to history. Anglo-Saxon jewellery comes in general from burials, the graves of its owners or from graves provided with family, official, and sometimes magically endowed treasures. There is thus no help to be obtained from sources available for the study of jewels of later periods as, for example, portraits, bills and accounts, inventories and design-books. In the main, though by no means exclusively, Anglo-Saxon jewels were designed for the practical use and adornment of women, as were the jewels of other periods of antiquity and indeed those of the present day. Many have long been known, but others are recent discoveries made by archaeologists and by chance in the daily happenings of agriculture and industry.

Also much to the point we can mark the real pleasure and delight with which the ordinary man becomes acquainted with the jewels of his early English forefathers, some named and known by their status, others as unknown as perhaps he himself. The immediate purpose of jewellery lies, of course, in its use of precious and rare materials for personal adornment, but we do well to adopt a wider viewpoint so as to include trinkets which in themselves are not precious either for the value of their material or the design and beauty of their workmanship. The plain and severe cruciform bronze brooch, the mass-produced ornament of the Anglian woman, has an interest of its own equal in degree, though obviously not in its richness and rareness, with the treasure of Sutton Hoo and with the sumptuous garnet-set and filigree-decorated gold brooches from Kent. It has been claimed that jewellery is in a sense the oldest art, but it is not only its age, its occasional richness and rareness, not even its magical or prophylactic or literary significance that gives Anglo-Saxon jewellery a wide appeal. It is in its own right an exciting personal discovery. This short book is an account of some aspects of such discovery, intended to interest the many, not to inform the select few. For readers who wish to know more about the historical background, the life of the ordinary people, of closely related arts, of other kinds of metalwork, of sculpture, architecture, and of manuscript art, a select bibliography is added. As some indication of the scope of Anglo-Saxon studies, it may be noted that the text accompanying the Ordnance Survey *Map of Britain in the Dark Ages* alone covers thirty-three major items.

There is another point to be borne in mind. The so-called Dark Ages, from AD 410 to 870, are becoming much lighter. Although the early mercenaries consisted of Angles, Saxons, and Jutes in various contemporary family and tribal connections, modern archaeology can now distinguish reasonably well between the relics of the Saxons of Essex, Sussex, and Wessex, the Middle Angles of Central England, the East Angles of Suffolk, the Mercians and the Northumbrians, and the inhabitants of the wealthy area of Kent who may not all have been Jutes. In this study details of common types of Anglian, Saxon, and Kentish brooches, jewellery available to people of all ranks and kinds, has played a leading part, and it is to this matter considered in its widest British and related continental contexts that many of the specialized works listed in the bibliography are devoted.

The author and publishers are greatly indebted to the museums who have so readily given permission for the illustration of objects in their collections for inclusion in this small book. The museums are named in the Notes on the Plates. Many museums now sell excellent postcards and coloured transparencies of objects in their own collections.

2

Discovery in the past

Since all archaeology depends in the first instance upon discovery, this book must start by considering the eventful story of the discovery of Anglo-Saxon jewellery in Britain, a few of its personalities, and the background against which it is set. There is discovery, too, in our own approach to this remarkable jewellery whether it be through the glass of a museum case or from the page of a book, and for this reason the bibliography is prefaced by a list of museums containing or exhibiting Anglo-Saxon jewellery.

Many discoveries have been made by sheer chance and indeed are often still made by ordinary people in the course of their daily work and during their leisure hours. There can be no better introduction to archaeology and no better way of realizing that the past lives in the present, for the jewellery in its various forms was valued and used by a wide variety of people. Occasionally even king and commoner meet almost face to face. Commoner met king one autumn day in 1780 at Laverstock (or Laverstoke) in Wiltshire when a carter glancing backward over his tracks saw the glitter of a gold finger-ring which by its inscription was later recognized as a possession of, or possibly a gift by, King Ethelwulf (836–58), father of Alfred the Great. A finely decorated and inscribed gold finger-ring belonging to his daughter Ethelswith (who in 853 married Burhred, King of Mercia) was found in 1870 near Aberford in the West Riding of Yorkshire by a ploughman who pulled it from the ground on the tip of his coulter. So little did he think of it that he tied it to the collar of his dog, and it was later exchanged by a jeweller in York for a set of tablespoons which the ploughman regarded as a more useful possession. Another gold finger-ring inscribed with the name of Alhstan, Bishop of Sherborne (823–67), was found near Colwyn Bay,

Denbighshire, by a farm labourer who for many years wore it to secure his own necktie. The chance discovery of what she called a 'curiosity', a piece of glittering metal in a bunch of sea-weed, made by a woman walking along the beach near Bacton, Norfolk, in the winter of 1845, led to the recognition of a fine garnet-decorated gold pendant set with a gold medallion, a copy of the *solidus* of the Emperor Mauricius and his colleague Theodosius (582—602) struck at Arles, a noteworthy piece of Anglo-Saxon jewellery. The world-famous gold and crystal-covered enamelled jewel bearing the name of King Alfred, a treasured possession of Oxford University for more than two hundred years, was a chance find dug up in Somerset close to Athelney, the Isle of the Nobles. One may also recall two chance finds of much less valuable pieces made in recent years by people with sharp eyes and their wits about them. A barmaid in an East Kent pub often wore with delight a fifth-century bronze brooch found near Lyminge by her father whilst dibbing cabbages and polished and given a new pin by her garage-apprentice brother. The remains of a Saxon hut uncovered by a boy of eleven in the back garden of his Hertfordshire home when his father had told him jokingly to go out and dig for treasure produced, among many other relics, pieces of bronze brooches.

Anglo-Saxon jewellery has been for the most part preserved because it formed part of the often elaborate decoration and equipment provided in their pagan graves to distinguish the wealthy, to appease the gods, and to ensure the needs of an after-life. Sometimes there was no luxury, and common-place, long-worn, and even jewellery that had apparently been discarded was chosen to be placed in the grave. Such pagan practices persisted to some degree though not perhaps with such a direct conscious meaning after the coming of Christianity. Fashions and beliefs did not change suddenly. So far as burial rites are concerned, cremation and inhumation often overlapped in pagan cemeteries. Pagan motifs in art may still have been used to express Christian beliefs and thoughts, and the spread of Christianity was neither rapid in fact nor uniform in progress. Like many other relics of antiquity pagan and Christian graves and their contents have often been uncovered by chance in building operations and the provision of utility services, in the always increasing quarrying for the raw materials used in building, especially in the valleys of the Thames, Trent, Ouse, Severn, and Welland, in new road works, in agriculture, especially in ploughing, and as the Saxons used river-systems for trade as well as invasion and settlement, relics of their travels and occupation have been found during dredging operations, river improvement works, even in fishing. The Thames from earliest times has been a main gateway from the Continent and at various points along its banks from the estuary almost to the headwaters the face of the land and the suitable character of the subsoil encouraged Saxon settlement. So too other river-systems gave access to regions well inland as did the extensive spread of Roman major and minor roads and canals, not all of which by any means had fallen into disuse.

Early discoveries of Anglo-Saxon jewellery made either by chance or by specific excavation have sometimes been recorded with effect. The stately prose of Sir Thomas Browne in his *Hydrotaphia, or Urn Burial* written in 1658 describes what we can quickly recognize as elaborately decorated cruciform or square-headed Anglian brooches from the cremation cemetery dug up at Old Walsingham in Norfolk. In 1730 an excavation party led by Cromwell Mortimer, a well-known antiquary who played an important part in the founding (or refounding) of the Society of Antiquaries in 1717, dug a series of burial mounds on the chalk downs of Chartham in East Kent. All were of Saxon date and the technical descriptions of the relics of which several versions were published, especially of the jewelled brooches, are excellent. The excavations were watched by a ten-year-old boy named Bryan Faussett who was later to distinguish himself as a zealous excavator in East Kent and to become the owner of the then finest collection of Anglo-Saxon antiquities. His museum was sold by his descendants to Joseph Mayer, a successful Liverpool businessman, who presented it to his native town where in the City Museum its fine jewellery, including the famous Kingston brooch, marks one of the most notable of all collections of Anglo-Saxon antiquities. Faussett made his explorations between 1757 and 1773 though his careful records, *Inventorium Sepulchrale*, were not published until 1856 under the editorship of another well-known antiquary, Charles Roach Smith. In recent years the whole collection has been re-examined and recorded by Mrs Sonia Chadwick Hawkes in the Institute of Archaeology in the University of Oxford, and her new publication which will shed much light on the Saxon occupation of East Kent and many other matters of moment is keenly awaited by archaeologists both here and on the Continent. In 1779 Captain James Douglas, later to take Holy Orders, then an ordnance engineer in charge of digging new fortification lines at Chatham to protect the Medway and the Dockyard against a possible invasion by the French, made remarkable discoveries of Anglo-Saxon remains, including much jewellery, which were to lay the foundations for a later study of pagan Saxondom in his book *Nenia Britannica* published in 1793. Most of Douglas's famous collection was bought from his widow by Sir Richard Colt Hoare, one of the first of the scientific excavators in Britain, and in 1829 he presented the larger part of it to the University of Oxford where it may now be seen in the Ashmolean Museum. And as one further example of the notable early excavators who took a special interest in Anglo-Saxon relics including jewellery, there may be quoted Thomas Bateman who in 1848 and again in 1861 recorded in two books the various excavations made by his family between 1820 and 1858, partly in Saxon barrows and in barrows containing secondary Saxon burials in Derbyshire, Staffordshire, and Yorkshire.

The eighteenth and nineteenth centuries saw a great increase in the number of antiquarians and collectors and there was constant inquiry and search to enrich their private display cases. It so happened that between the years 1860 and 1894 there arrived in Kent what was in more senses than one a golden opportunity. The London, Chatham, and Dover Railway was extended close to Faversham across an area known, it was said from time immemorial, as King's Field, part no doubt of the *villa regis* of Faversham which from the opening years of the ninth century was important enough to be slowly partitioned among powerful courtiers and churchmen. The railway was some years in construction and there followed extensive digging for brick-earth at the side of the line during all of which time there were frequent discoveries of Saxon relics and particularly of fine jewellery. Collectors and their agents both English and foreign offered large prices to the poorly paid railway navvies and it is frankly impossible to say what was discovered and whether the many hundreds of relics came from graves or from unrecognized domestic or perhaps trading settlements. William Gibbs, a retired grocer of Faversham, had acquired some 2,500 beads alone when his sumptuous collection was bequeathed to the British Museum in 1870, to say nothing of many pieces of magnificent jewellery. To what extent the landowners, other collectors, and the wealthy secretive collectors who would permit no reference whatever to their private museums benefited, can only be judged in part by reference to sale catalogues of later days. But the name of the King's Field is a true reflection of its importance against which could be set some of the richest Saxon jewels ever to be discovered. The fashion of antiquarian digging at this time is well set by the excavation in 1883 of a remarkable burial-mound then in the old churchyard at Taplow, Buckinghamshire, and now within private grounds adjoining Taplow Court. It contained the burial of a chieftain, presumably the *Taeppa* after whom the *hlāw* or burial-mound was named, with his full armoury, fine glassware, an Egyptian bronze bowl, drinking horns, gaming-pieces, a lyre, and a set of magnificent gold buckles, his body being wrapped in gold embroidered clothing and laid with the head to the east. These relics, too, are fortunately on exhibition in the British Museum.

3

Discovery in the present

In 1939 one of the most spectacular and important discoveries known to British archaeology was made at Sutton Hoo in Suffolk. It was nothing less than the funeral monument of a Saxon king of the seventh century, probably, it seems, Raedwald of East Anglia who died in 625 or 626. A large rowing boat had been pulled up from the sea and sunk into the ground, and after a wooden burial-chamber or mausoleum had been built almost amidships the whole structure was covered with a mound, one of a number in the same small area. In the wooden chamber which had collapsed under the great weight of the mound was the richest funeral treasure ever to be found in Britain. It included personal weapons and armour with Swedish affinities, fine jewellery, a remarkable stone sceptre, thirty-seven Merovingian gold coins with the better part of a magnificently jewelled purse, a collection of exotic pieces of silver plate, drinking horns, a lyre, and a wealth of domestic apparatus. Such a brief summary must serve for our present purpose. After a special coroner's inquest on the discovery, the landowner, the late Mrs E. M. Pretty, who had sponsored an investigation of the site, was held to be the owner of the treasure which, with unbounded public spirit, she then gave to the nation, making to the British Museum one of the most splendid gifts ever to be received in a donor's lifetime. Specialists working under the threat of approaching war and under most difficult practical conditions excavated the ship-burial and the site was again examined in 1967–9 under controlled conditions. Full details together with the results of new and long examination and new reconstructions of certain of these important remains will soon appear in a series of definitive publications by the British Museum. The Sutton Hoo research team at the Museum, brilliantly led by

Dr R. L. S. Bruce-Mitford and supported by his colleagues in the research laboratory and by other experts, has already produced a new understanding of this unique discovery which Sir Thomas Kendrick, one of our leading Anglo-Saxon scholars, described as 'the most marvellous find in the archaeological annals of England'. Indeed there had been nothing like it since the fortunate chance finding in 1653 of a brilliant treasure in the grave of the Frankish king Childeric I (d. 481) at Tournai in Belgium, most of which was stolen in 1831 from the famous royal Cabinet des Medailles in Paris. Later in this book we shall describe some outstanding examples of the remarkable locally made jewellery from this royal ship-burial, a memorial of an East Anglian king.

In recent years the excavation and adequate recording of sites of archaeological interest threatened by immediate destruction from mineral working, housing and industrial development, and road construction has been a constant concern of the Department of the Environment and of many archaeological bodies, national and local. Among these sites are several of post-Roman and medieval date which have yielded jewellery of special interest either from its own character, its wider cultural significance or its association with other relics of the same periods. There are obviously other good reasons for excavation, and as a measure of interest in this period it may be noted that some fifty English sites are noted in the Pre-Conquest section of the summary *Medieval Britain* published in the 1970 volume of *Medieval Archaeology*, the journal of the Society for Medieval Archaeology. A very brief outline of this valuable and generally well-conducted research is all that can be attempted here. It should be noted in passing that visitors cannot usually be accepted on an excavation site without prior arrangement and that many of the objects discovered, pieces of jewellery among them, are not available for general viewing until they have been adequately cleaned, studied, and possibly published. The story of the past belongs to Everyman as all field archaeologists recognize to the full, but their work in its exploration and elucidation must proceed unhindered as far as possible.

Among these are Mucking, Thurrock, in **Essex** where on a site occupied since the early Bronze Age no less than 102 sunken Saxon huts (*grubenhäuser*) and two cemeteries have yielded jewellery such as disc-brooches (the various types of jewellery are described in full in a later chapter of this book) a claw-shaped pendant with an intaglio of blue paste, a seventh-century silver pin inlaid with garnet, a penannular brooch with zoomorphic terminals, shale bracelets, amber and clear and polychrome glass beads, in addition to the more usual equipment of clay weights for a weaving loom, iron slag, and pieces of domestic pottery. The cemeteries associated with the settlement were extensive and one, possibly a complete cemetery and therefore a rare occurrence, contained more than 600 burials. Cremation and inhumation were practised at the same time and often on the same sites. The list of jewellery is formidable even in summary and its full study will add much to our knowledge. It includes disc, saucer, square-headed, equal-armed, applied, annular, and penannular or broken ring brooches with one brooch of an outstandingly interesting Scandinavian type, a rare form of North Gaulish plate-brooch of which only two other examples, both from Kent, are known. There were also strings of amber, crystal, and glass beads with some 160 beads on one necklace, and rare segmented glass beads. A woman's inhumation burial contained a string of 91 beads associated with a pair of square-headed and a pair of saucer brooches, together with a silver finger-ring, and at her feet a pair of domestic shears and a glass bowl. The graves also contained other relics indicative of the occupations, hopes, and beliefs of those so buried: impressions of linen and woollen garments on objects of bronze and iron, swords, spears, a knife and shield-bosses, a bronze-bound bucket decorated with masks of human faces, and with certain cremations, tweezers, buckles, and beads. One quite exceptional discovery made in 1967 in a man's grave was a fine set of five pieces of belt-furnishings intricately decorated and inlaid with silver. Nearly all this exceptionally well-directed excavation work on the seaward-riverside edge of a gravel terrace has been undertaken by the Ancient Monuments Branch of the Department of the Environment with the support of the Mucking Excavation Committee in advance of commercial gravel quarrying. It is a remarkable achievement over some six or seven years, directed by Mrs M. U. Jones.

In **Kent** at Finglesham near Deal excavations by Mrs Sonia Chadwick Hawkes between 1959 and 1967 revealed 216 graves with 11 barrow-burials, the majority belonging to the seventh and early eighth centuries. In earlier years the graves of a wealthy family with striking sixth-century jewellery had been uncovered, but only two such graves now remained. One of a man contained a silver garnet-set Frankish buckle, and that of a woman had four silver brooches, a couple of silver pins, garnet-set belt-fittings, and a triple necklace of amber, glass, gold, and silver beads and gold pendants. 'The Finglesham Man' figured on a gilt bronze buckle from grave 95 has become deservedly famous.

Near Broadstairs some 388 burials of the late sixth to the early eighth centuries were found not to be especially well furnished, though previous discoveries nearby had disclosed the existence of a rich cemetery which had been robbed in antiquity. Imported Frankish pottery and palisaded ditches defining walled and stone-lined graves were new features confirmed in 1970 by Chatham House Grammar School Archaeological Society in its three-season quest started after a chance find as a council rubbish tip was being extended. The human remains from this cemetery are receiving close professional study which will certainly disclose information about the diet, health, and general living conditions of these Saxon inhabitants of East Kent, as will recent discoveries on the site of the North Sea gas pipeline in Thanet.

At Dover in 1972 archaeologists found a garnet-set gold finger-ring, one of the finest pieces of Saxon jewellery yet found in the country.

Road developments at Polhill, Dunton Green, chiefly in 1964–7, revealed a large cemetery of the late seventh and early eighth centuries which contained a variety of ornaments and accessories which have been fully published by the Kent Archaeological Rescue Unit.

In **Norfolk** at North Elmham the skilled excavation in 1970 of the sites of thirty timber buildings of the seventh to the twelfth centuries revealed no jewellery whatever.

At Wakerley, **Northamptonshire**, in 1970 more than 400 objects recovered from 85 burials included 74 brooches of types already well-known in sixth-century Midlands archaeological contexts. In due course they will be exhibited at Westfield Museum, Kettering.

In the same year, in 367 urns excavated at Newark, **Nottinghamshire**, under the auspices of Nottingham University, there appears to have been but one large crystal bead and pieces of a saucer brooch.

In **Suffolk** at West Stow a settlement of 60 huts dating it seems from the fifth to the seventh centuries and demarked by boundary ditches, excavated in 1970 by Bury St Edmunds Council Museum, produced one very unusual iron brooch of a late fourth-century continental type which will be bound to arouse much interest in due course.

In **Warwickshire** three Anglo-Saxon sites in danger have been excavated in recent years by the Avon–Severn Valleys Research Project, the Stratford Society, and Warwick County Museum. We can mention here only the jewellery discovered. At Stretton under Fosse sunken huts contained a cross potent, trefoil, disc, saucer, and square-headed brooches of bronze, necklaces of glass beads and six discs from shield-bosses, with decoration in applied gold and silver. A pagan cemetery at Stratford-upon-Avon contained silver penannular and applied brooches, while at Bidford-on-Avon one woman was inhumed with her very rich possessions.

These are but very brief notes of discovery by purpose. Often, as in Canterbury for example, the redevelopment of Victorian and Edwardian building has destroyed all vestiges of Saxon traces above the levels of Roman occupation, and only seldom can discovery be made by a set programme of excavation. But from time to time discovery of Anglo-Saxon as of other antiquities is still made by chance, though not perhaps as frequently. Several noteworthy casual finds have already been mentioned, but one other recent example deserves notice here. In Kent, in 1967, a farm-worker at Thurnham found a Saxon gold cross of quality whilst he was harrowing a field and it was lost again after it dropped off his tractor, only to be rediscovered by a friend. This fine seventh-century pectoral cross was set with a central and lateral garnets in beaded gold thread imitating filigree work, a notable piece of jeweller's work of its kind. The jury at a special coroner's inquest decided by eight votes to one that the cross had been lost by someone unknown, and it was therefore not treasure trove and not the property of the Crown. At a subsequent auction it was sold for £5,000.

One other means of discovering the nature and importance of Anglo-Saxon jewellery, and, of course, other objects of archaeological interest, is often overlooked. This is the recognition and identification of pieces long since forgotten which appear at a sale room or occasionally in a little-consulted museum store, and the new appreciation of features, usually decorative, on jewels already well-known. An outstanding example in the first class was the simultaneous but independent recognition of the once famous but long-lost Sutton, Isle of Ely, disc-brooch by Dr R. L. S. Bruce-Mitford and the present writer; of the second, Mr George Speake's interesting suggestion that the well-known gold coin pendant from Bacton, Norfolk, is a product of the Sutton Hoo workshop, as indeed may be the gold garnet-set pendant with a coin of the Byzantine Emperor Heraclius (610–41) from Wilton, Norfolk.

4
Materials and techniques

The materials and technical processes used by the makers of Anglo-Saxon jewellery must now be considered.

The essential metals were gold, silver, and bronze.

In early times Roman **gold** came from Arabia, but especially from Spain where there was a well-established industry. Its qualities were obvious: it was imperishable, it bought luxuries from the East, it was ostentatious, and it was lasting. Of the very small quantity of gold produced in Roman Britain and of the metal imported, especially in the form of coins or medallions, little is likely to have been preserved and that chiefly perhaps by hoarding. The re-use of prehistoric gold objects discovered by chance is no more than an interesting possibility. There were larger and more accessible supplies to be obtained in the provinces of the Later Empire, where by its extensive use enemies were subsidized, mercenaries paid, and barbarian intruders bought off. The Goths in their path across Europe had left a plentiful supply of gold behind them. By the end of the fifth century AD the Visigoths in Spain and the Burgundians in France were using gold coinage, and from the early part of the sixth century gold of the Merovingian Franks travelled from Marseilles by the Rhône Valley to Paris and the Middle Rhine and so to the shores of the English Channel. It is interesting to reflect that such gold could have contained metal derived ultimately from Eastern or Egyptian treasures, from earlier Roman coins and jewellery, even from gold coins of the Greeks. The fact that gold coins of the Early Empire reached India in some quantity is an additional comment on the nature of the trade. One has only to look at the wide range of colour in a series of gold Saxon jewels to see at once that whatever its treatment in the melting-pot and subsequently by the jeweller the metal is derived from a variety of sources. Modern metallurgical techniques are likely to produce interesting results in such an inquiry into this special aspect of archaeology and history as they have already done in the study of coins. Gold as a metal had many advantages. It could be hammered cold, it could be worked relatively easily, chased and engraved, soldered rather than rivetted, and wafer-thin it could be stamped in relief. Beyond these special advantages to the jeweller it was decorative, had a positive beauty, was rare, and with its imperishable quality had a special nature, and was an outstanding emblem of wealth and power.

Beaten metal was the foundation of most of the gold jewellery, whether rings, pendants, or brooches, and cut into strips, bent into cloisons, open or covered, of circular, rectangular, mushroom, honeycomb, cusped, and multiple-step patterns (in the Sutton Hoo jewellery it is possible to identify no less than nineteen or twenty different cell-forms), all of which could be enriched with semi-precious stones, fine coloured glass and enamels, it exhibited a superb control maintained by the worker. Only occasionally does one see the handiwork of an apprentice, even of a journeyman, and is seems possible that pieces which did not reach a satisfactory standard were melted down and the materials reused on another occasion.

But it is in his delicate handling of threaded, beaded, pearled, and braided gold wire and in its adaptation to filigree of both simple and intricate patterns of interlace and in granulation that the Saxon worker excelled. Whether it was hammered and rolled or occasionally made by means of a draw-plate, twisted and coiled wire was often used to give delicacy to a hard edge, especially on gold pendants, and by the use of plait the Saxon jeweller was able to produce the shadow light-and-dark effect which, beginning with the chip-carving technique copied from Germanic wood-working (and even imbued perhaps with ideas from as far afield as Greece and Italy), was as early as the fifth century one of the canons of his art. In the shape and curves of some gold pieces there is an English idiom in which Celtic reversion played an important part, but Frankish, Gothic, Langobard, and Scandinavian, particularly Danish and Swedish, ideas also influenced the design and execution of motifs which included human, animal and naturalistic themes. The use of *cloisonné* came originally from

Egypt and the East in the days of far antiquity. In the seventh century when some gold work and jewellery was confined to the remote workshops of the church, craftsmanship could become conservative: compare, for example, the pectoral cross of St Cuthbert (*c.* 687), with its poor workmanship, clumsy repair, and reused material with the luminosity, gracefulness, and elegance of the Kentish jewelled brooches and the regal treasures of Sutton Hoo belonging to the earlier part of the same century. Always it must be borne in mind that most jewellery was intended for personal ornament chiefly for women, but other pieces such as sword-mounts and belt-fittings were designed and produced for ceremonial use, even as the insignia of a king or chieftain.

The brilliant lustre of **silver** and its great ductile and malleable qualities made it a favourite precious metal of the Saxon jeweller. It had been an extensive official export from Roman Britain; the mines which were the chief source of its supply were working as late as the fourth century and it seems likely that there must have been some metal still available apart from the hoards of plate which early marauding bands of Saxon pirates would make it their business to obtain. Looting raids furnished treasure which could be consigned to the melting-pot, but later jewellers and moneyers used silver in ingots, some of it specially imported.

The Saxon craftsmen cast the framework of many of their silver brooches and such attachments as buckle-plates, strap-ends, and fasteners for the cuff. Sometimes the piece was beaten up from a flat cast. Rings, bangles, and bracelets were made from both wire and strip. Decoration was incised, traced, or stamped or sometimes worked in *repoussé*; filigree was used and cast jewels were brightened by chasing and often by gilding. Plates or discs of embossed silver were frequently applied to brighten brooches of simply cast bronze. Again the contrast between light and shade, of much appeal to Teutonic craftsmen whose past traditions were in part laid in woodcraft, was secured by filling incised lines of a pattern on silver with niello, a black paste consisting (at least until about the eleventh century as Dr A. A. Moss has demonstrated) of a silver sulphide which was heated after its infilling and then burnished, and sometimes by gilding with a thin skin of gold which was afterwards highly polished. As decorative processes, both were extremely effective.

Of the third metal, **bronze**, there were adequate supplies in the sub-Roman world. Much of the material used by the Saxon craftsmen for their brooches, rings, and bracelets was probably obtained from the melting down of Roman coins, trinkets, and bowls, and badly damaged pieces from their own stocks in trade were no doubt treated in the same way. The density and hardness of bronze allows it to take the form of any mould however delicate, and by the lost-wax process Saxon jewellers were able to produce remarkable pieces of solid casting over a long period of time. The lost wax or *cire-perdue* process is an old-established method of casting in which the wax model round a core is melted by the metal which at once replaces it. Many people find it difficult to follow a description of the process on paper: Cellini's account of his Perseus in the *Life lxxv–lxxviii* is as good as and certainly far more entertaining than any other. There is also an informative exhibition of the process in the new Department of Ethnology of the British Museum at Burlington Gardens, London W1.

The general standard of bronze-casting, though it may suggest something like mass-production, is almost uniformly good. None but satisfactory pieces were retained for the carefully carried out process of finishing, a practice which seems scarcely to accord with the pathetic efforts so often made to repair jewels of small intrinsic but obviously sentimental worth. Details of the casting work are unknown. Not a single jewellery mould whether of clay or wood has been discovered, but judging from the impressions left on several roughly finished brooches, clay or a fine facing sand may have been used. Experiments made some years ago by the writer using sand from the Thanet Beds in North Kent and bronze from some indecipherable Third Brass Roman coins of no known location gave excellent results with the ordinary cruciform pattern brooch. In addition to the lost-wax and other moulds there must have been many shallow open moulds, possibly even of stone, in which some of the best large square-headed brooches were cast. Sometimes it is possible to recognize brooches which have been cast from the same mould such as the remarkable pair from Londesborough, in the East Riding of Yorkshire, now in Hull Museum. An interesting recent discovery was that a cruciform brooch from Ixworth, Suffolk, acquired in 1927 by the British

Museum, came from the same mould as a brooch which was acquired in 1971 as of unknown provenance. Both are technically of brass, with stylized horses' heads as decoration and traces of enamel which originally relieved the dot-and-circle patterns on the head-plates.

Bronze jewels were decorated by much the same technical processes as those of silver, but the very nature of the pieces with their cleverly balanced masses, their mouldings, facets, and interplay of plane surfaces often made an imposed decoration unnecessary. Gilding and attached silver plaques provided a popular finish and there was always the hard trim glitter of the newly polished metal itself, the poorer man's gold.

Iron is scarcely used except for an occasional belt-buckle, though the brooch from West Stow, Suffolk, already mentioned shows the possibilities of this metal. The use of **pewter** is not common. Brooches of this alloy are in the main poorly designed apart from the disc variety with scroll pattern decoration in vogue during the ninth, tenth, and eleventh centuries. The best-known brooch of pewter, one found in the City of London and now in the British Museum, is of better workmanship than the general run; it is decorated with a backward-looking lion within a pearled border and the surface bears traces of its one-time gilding.

Iron and bronze buckle-loops, occasionally brooches and strap-mounts (and weapons which, in general, are beyond the scope of this book) were sometimes decorated with inlays of silver or bronze wire or with plates or small sheets of these metals. In a detailed examination of early Anglo-Saxon inlaid metalwork Miss Vera Evison points out that this material increases in the fifth century with *repoussé* plate buckles which are found on both sides of the Channel and on bronze objects with strong Roman influence in their design. There are others which represent an individual insular development associated with northern and continental antecedents. The craft declined towards the end of the sixth century, it seems, but late in the succeeding century, Miss Evison emphasizes, it showed fresh ideas and a complete mastery of execution. This clever study made in 1955 is an outstanding example of the kind of specialized work that is necessary, though for long neglected by archaeologists, for a more complete understanding of the stylistic background of particular types of

Anglo-Saxon jewellery.

There are records of one or two pieces of **bone** which can be accepted as jewellery, a buckle, a finger-ring, and an annular brooch, all unattractive objects and possibly trial pieces for later styles of metalwork.

Ivory rings, some clearly bracelets, others the framework of fabric purses or of chatelaines for keys and small workboxes, are not uncommon in the graves of Saxon women. The sources of the ivory and its long journey to Britain in the course of trade are fascinating problems in themselves. The chatelaines recall the Roman matron's comparable symbols of her status and duties.

The stone in greatest demand was **garnet**, and its fine red glow on a background of gold, a brave show, provided an outstanding feature of the setting for the best of the late sixth- and early seventh-century polychrome jewels. The garnet was cut, sometimes round in cabochon, that is polished but not faceted, its brilliance often being heightened by a setting in pricked or cross-hatched gold foil. Almandine, the deep red precious garnet, originally from India, was abundant enough in the luxury trade of Roman times, and its spread across Europe can be seen in Teutonic treasures from the Eastern Mediterranean, Italy, Central Europe, Belgium, Sweden, and Kent. The masterly Kentish style of jewellery typified above all by the famous polychrome gold and garnet-encrusted brooches from Kingston and Sarre must now give place in brilliance and technique to the jewellery from the treasure of the Sutton Hoo ship-burial. In all, the Sutton Hoo jewels are decorated with more than 4,000 garnets, each cut individually. We can as yet only wonder how and under what physical and technical conditions the jewellers worked.

In place of garnet a fine red glass is sometimes used, and indeed the recent highly scientific investigations of Dr G. F. Claringbull have shown that it is blue glass, and not lapis lazuli as was previously thought, that provides the fine contrast to the overwhelming red filling of the cloisons in the famous jewelled brooches of Kentish type. And at Sutton Hoo, as Dr R. L. S. Bruce-Mitford has pertinently said, *millefiori* glass (that is ornamental glass rods of varying colours and diameters which have been fused together and afterwards stretched and cut into small sections) in the form of blue and white or red and white chequers 'appears for the first time in Germanic jewellery, and at the highest level, in the garnet-encrusted gold jewels that are the richest relics of the pagan Saxons, and in the making of which Saxon goldsmiths exerted their highest skill.'

There is also in some of the early ornate Kentish brooches a contrasting background of white inlay. It has been generally described as of shell or meerschaum, bone or ivory, but modern examination by X-ray diffraction of the white inlays of eight Kentish brooches in the British Museum suggests that the jewellers may have used any white stone-like material at hand. Ivory which appears in other jewellery was certainly available, but as Miss Evison rightly says in her account of this problem, further and wider investigation is still needed.

Amber, a yellowish fossil resin washed out of extinct pine forests on to the Baltic shores and to the coasts of East Anglia, was often quite skilfully worked, faceted, and polished into beads. Among its ancient prophylactic virtues was a defence against witchcraft which may have commended it to a people whose lives were conditioned by trolls and gremlins. It is possible that East Anglia may have developed a short-lived amber trade of its own in the second half of the sixth century, but a well-recognized amber trade by way of the Baltic and the Danube had existed in the days of early prehistory.

Amethyst, a transparent purple or violet quartz, was used with a remarkable skill in piercing and polishing in the making of beads, eardrops, and as a principal pendant in necklaces. Often necklaces are made up of many finely made pear-shaped beads, expertly matched and graded, luxury possessions which also had a charm in giving protection against drunkenness which may have appealed to the Saxon mind. The ultimate source was the eastern Mediterranean, but many of the amethyst beads found in the graves of wealthy Kentish women came from Frankish tribes in the Rhineland and may have been loot from Roman sources.

Jewellery of **agate** and **onyx** is rare. Skilfully cut beads of **rock-crystal** found sometimes in men's graves may represent sword-knots, and there have been suggestions that crystal and enamel may have taken the place of gold when the use of gold or precious stones may have become restricted through economic reasons, though such a theory has obvious drawbacks.

Beads are readily carried over long distances. They are practically indestructible although easily lost under ordinary conditions of life. Those of precious materials must have been valued possessions, heirlooms even, and beads are one of the most persistent and widespread forms of popular art. It does not seem beyond the realms of possibility that beads to the Anglo-Saxon weaver had something of the same sort of significance as did the beads on the bobbins of some English and Maltese lace-makers a generation ago when on a death one bobbin was preserved with a bead for each year of the worker's life as a commemoration. But on any count Anglo-Saxon beads had a very long life, and their distribution and form has received more than one detailed expert consideration. Clear, opaque, and coloured glass in the form of cylinders, spheres, discs, cubes, and bugles, chevron beads of red, white, and blue glass cane cut into a biconoid form, beads of gilded glass, others with polychrome and mosaic inlays certainly give rise to acute problems in archaeology and in chronology, but to many people their sheer variety alone is a quite outstanding discovery.

At the risk of over-simplification a few words must be said about Anglo-Saxon jewellery as an art. This involved and highly specialized study has been the subject of more than one long book and of many detailed contributions to learned journals. The techniques used in the decoration of jewellery are both simple and involved. In pagan times, as we have noted, chip-carving, an imitation of the Germanic carving of hard wood by Roman and sub-Roman metalworkers, was extensively used. The rich gold and silver *cloisonné* jewellery inlaid with garnets, glass, and other material and decorated with filigree has been recognized by archaeologists for many years, but the Sutton Hoo discovery has added (among many other matters) the background of specialized East Anglian workshops to the already well-known jewels from Kent. The art forms and subjects of decoration can for simplicity be recognized as animal ornament, sometimes abstract and quite unreal, and schemes of simple or involved linear pattern. The use of animal ornament was an involved legacy from Classical and Germanic sources which came, diffused by way of trade or even by military service, via Eastern Europe, the Rhineland, and Scandinavia. Several animal styles can be distinguished, and there is an interlacing ribbon-ornament with animals and plant tendrils, knotted and looped patterns often displaying a strong element of symmetry which may have been derived from Italy or from Baltic regions. The two main styles are sometimes combined in greater or lesser degree, and animal styles are often made in a chip-carving technique so as to cover a whole surface. Art forms which came from the Continent with the first arrivals were, after their adoption in Britain, influenced in their turn and over many years by Germanic and Scandinavian examples. In the same way, some of the ideas and skills of the jewellers in Britain found their way in modified form back to the Continent.

The advent of Christianity did not make any radical change in the technique and art forms of Anglo-Saxon jewellery. As we have already seen the early seventh-century jewellers in East Anglia made outstandingly notable pieces of *cloisonné,* and the Christian jeweller made his religious pectoral crosses using much the same techniques as his pagan brethren. Chip-carving and a more naturalistic interlacing, scroll-patterns, and a variety of leaf and plant patterns continued to be used. By the end of the ninth century gold supplies were becoming restricted and an Age of Silver with fine animal ornament carved on mounts, disc-brooches, and ecclesiastical objects had already ensured that the Anglo-Saxon jeweller was an artist in his own right who occupied a prominent and effective place in the wide background of Europe. His later attempts to use the famous Ringerike and Jellinge styles of Viking craftsmen cannot be followed in this book, but something of his achievement can be seen in the Sutton, Isle of Ely, disc-brooch.

Many details of the life of Anglo-Saxon peoples have been revealed by careful excavation of their settlements in recent years. There is evidence enough of sheep-rearing, spinning and weaving, of potter's workshops, tools, and gear, of industrial rubbish-pits, sometimes of iron-making, very often of remarkable timber buildings, halls, and houses; nowhere, it seems, has the undoubted workshop of a jeweller come to light. At Winchester, a small heavily gilt silver belt-plate decorated with chip-carving ornament possibly came from a noble grave of late Saxon date and it could have been made nearby. There was no indication of a jeweller's workshop at Yeavering in Northumberland, the site of King

Edwin's palace until his defeat about 633. Occasionally in a deserted medieval village such as Goltho, Lincolnshire, notable pieces of jewellery come to light, but it is not until late medieval times, as in Bristol and Winchester, that evidence of commercial bronze-working, and by inference possibly of jewellery-making, has been found. The workshops of the famous Kentish jewellers were destroyed without recognition by the Faversham railway workers and the subsequent brick-earth diggers. It is much to be hoped that one at least may yet be located by the experienced field archaeologists now working in the area. There is also hope that the seventh-century Saxon village now being excavated at Chalton, Hampshire, may among its timber houses and the one pit-house so far discovered include some part of a jeweller's premises. For the rest, all that we can point to are bronze scales and associated weights often adapted from Roman coins, equipment such as might be used by jewellers and goldsmiths, found in a few early graves in East Kent. The life of the jewellers and their process of work, by daylight or by artificial light, still remain to be discovered. Of one thing we can be certain: brilliant jewellery such as the Kingston and Sarre Amherst brooches was not the product of an insecure society.

5
The jewels

For the present purpose it is most convenient to arrange a commentary on jewels with reference to the place in which they were worn on the human body. Thus we shall start with head-wear, then consider necklaces, beads, and pendants and so pass on to the very large groups of brooches and pins, to the jewelled decoration of belts, girdles, and some military equipment, to armlets and finger-rings, and so at last to the rare anklets. One or two of our world-famous Anglo-Saxon treasures will be specially noted, but it is not within the scope of this small book to include Viking and later jewellery in its full ranges, or indeed to comment upon, and illustrate, every variety and fashion in Anglo-Saxon jewellery.

The head jewels worn by women include brooches and pins worn to secure the hood, hair-pins, and ear-rings.

Hood-brooches and **pins** were decorative as well as practical, some of the former being perforated so that they could be more permanently attached to the fabric. Cloth-of-gold hoods or the gold braid edging to hoods are occasionally found in the graves of the wealthy, both male and female.

Hair-pins of metal and bone show, as might be expected in view of their widely spread origins, great variety in design and workmanship. There are small pins of bronze and of silver with simply moulded heads, and others in which the shaft is twisted or decorated and gilded and the head set with amethyst, garnet, or glass. Large and elaborate pins are sometimes of silver, often of gilded bronze, with plain or decorated disc-heads in the plane of the shaft. Ornate pins are often flat and plain on the underside as if they were worn in a 'bun' at the back of the head. There is a group of variously ornamented and sometimes gilded pins, the length and weight of which preclude their being hair or hood ornaments; their use is hard to explain except upon the votive or magic grounds sometimes assigned to rather similar decorated nails of Roman provenance. A hair-braid embroidered with pearls and silver thread in the Mayer Collection in the City of Liverpool Museum said to have been found in a Saxon grave in Kent seems to be unique, though it is worth while recalling that the warrior buried in the Taplow barrow had a gold binding to his tunic and gold was used fairly often in the hair-braids of women in East Kent.

It is certain from the wide prevalence of **ear-rings** that the hair was not worn so as to cover the ears. From evidence which James Douglas found in a barrow in Greenwich Park, Kent, in 1784 one woman dressed her fine auburn hair in plaits over her head which was covered with a coarse woollen hood, not a burial-shroud, decorated with coloured glass beads of quality. It is possible, though exact evidence is lacking, that ear-rings were sometimes worn by men. In general the Saxon woman was content with the simplest of ear-rings. The usual form is a small ring of plain thinly drawn silver wire which may have an adjustable slip-knot and which carries a bead or beads of blue or red glass, paste, or rather exceptionally of amethyst. Sometimes the silver wire is drawn to simulate filigree beading, and the ring may carry a spangle, plain or cut, with an open star. A larger variety of these 'knot-rings' were sometimes worn as necklaces, and they have a wide southern and Midland geographical distribution. Ear-rings with pendants are not common. Fine gold and jewel-set ear-rings in the continental Langobard and Merovingian fashion do not seem to have reached Britain but some of the more unusual kinds of metal beads, the precise original position of which in the grave is not now known, are possibly ear ornaments.

Necklaces are common features of the Anglo-Saxon woman's jewellery. They range in quality and workmanship from the rare and splendid gold and garnet sets as at Desborough, Northamptonshire, to the more usual necklaces composed of shaped amethyst, glass, and occasional amber beads, the materials of which we have already noticed. Such beads were also worn as waist-girdles and in strings and festoons on the breast hanging necklace-fashion from the neck or fastened by pairs of shoulder-brooches, decorative pins, or even sewn to the dress. In date these necklaces cover a vast range of time from the early days of pagan Saxondom onwards and they are still found in burials dating long after the Conversion. It is interesting to note that they are all archaeological discoveries, for such necklaces are not featured in manuscripts.

What seems to be a necklace or a collar for a child, found at Emscote, Warwickshire, and now in the British Museum, is of thin silver with a simple hooked fastening, and partly twisted yoke cleverly beaten out to make a broad collar which has an engraved zoomorphic pattern.

Pendants worn round the neck and pectoral jewels for the breast include those worn as charms or amulets, others which include coins and in particular the looped and coin-like discs known as bracteates, and the decorative pendants of glass mosaic, of silver, and of gold with jewelled and glass *cloisonné.*

Among the amulets or pieces of occult medicine are large cowrie shells from the Indian Ocean, items in an Eastern trade evidenced also by Coptic bronze bowls, glass from Egypt, and garnets from India. The shape and one of its names, *Concha veneris*, indicates sufficiently its prophylactic purposes, but some Christian women perhaps relied on an older superstition to protect themselves from 'overlooking'. Fossil shells, treasured perhaps as charms, and teeth of beaver, wolf, and horse, either mounted or pierced for suspension, are not uncommon. The latter may be trophies of the chase, but almost any bright trifle or antique was likely to be of use, even the enamelled scutcheon of a bronze hanging-bowl.

Pendants which include gold coins or medallions are among the best-known of our Saxon jewels. Those from Bacton and Wilton, Norfolk, and Forsbrook, North Staffordshire, contain Roman and Byzantine gold coins which, like the coins in the necklace from Sarre, provide some indication of date and are pertinent reminders that to the jeweller any roundel of gold, whatever its source, was an attractive centre-piece. The famous pectoral cross of St Cuthbert who died in 687 shows how the pagan style of garnet-set jewellery flourished in the church long after the Conversion, and other pendants including those already noted raise most interesting possibilities of comparisons with Romano-Celtic,

Gothic, and Classical treasures from which the techniques and designs of the rich polychrome jewellery of pagan Kent and East Anglia may have been ultimately derived in far antiquity. More must be said on this matter when we consider the polychrome brooches and the outstandingly magnificent jewellery from the Sutton Hoo ship-burial. Meanwhile we can but speculate with interest upon the source and subsequent story of gold coins and whether it was by way of trade or plunder or sheer accident of circumstances that they arrived in their well-to-do owner's possession.

Bracteates, thin circular gold pendants embossed with human and zoomorphic designs, have a loop for suspension and were worn as part of a necklace or as pendants by themselves. The decoration, always stamped from a die and more than one from the same die have been discovered, is a remote and fantastic imitation of late Roman gold coins and presentation medallions which were subsidies to the barbarians of northern Europe far beyond the frontiers of the Empire. From Scandinavia and particularly from Denmark some bracteates reached Britain just after the middle of the sixth century.

Pins of metal and of bone were common dress-fastenings for men and women of all classes throughout the Saxon period. The pin, an invention of early prehistoric times, showed in the Saxon ages a very wide variety of form, size, and decoration. There are silver and bronze 'spangled' pins, pins with decorated circular and disc heads, silver pins with expanding-ring heads, with garnets, paste, and glass beads at the head and pins with simple plainly moulded heads. Forms in bone are usually simple. One or two outstanding pins of silver and finely gilded bronze must by their size and the quality of their workmanship indicate something of their owner's rank. It is not always easy to decide the real purpose of a pin from its form alone. Its position in a grave is likewise no certain guide, for hair-pins were used to fasten hoods under the chin and where grave-shrouds were in fashion they were likely to be secured by any pin of suitable size. For burial purposes either a fine pin or one of little value might be selected.

Pin-suites, two or sometimes three pins linked by a chain or more rarely by a small plate, were worn both on the breast and in the hair. Those of gold set with garnets, of which there are fine examples in the British Museum from Little Hampton, Worcestershire, and in Devizes Museum from Roundway Down, Wiltshire, are purely decorative. Others, especially the paired suites, were cloak or tunic fasteners. Most famous of all is a linked set of three circular silver-gilt pins decorated with an intricate interlaced pattern in chip-carving, the eyes of its curious animal forms being originally inlaid with blue glass or paste. They were discovered during a spell of particularly dry weather in 1826 during improvements to the course of the River Witham near Fiskerton, Lincolnshire. This eighth-century ornament, precious enough to have been repaired by an Anglo-Saxon jeweller, was a particularly appropriate gift to have been made to the British Museum by the Royal Archaeological Institute.

Brooches are the most common pieces of Anglo-Saxon jewellery. They were worn as practical dress-fastenings by many people of all ranks and callings over a long period of time. The great number of brooches now known is impressive enough to have attracted the attention of many typologists and may now perhaps be studied statistically and by matrix analysis, a modern process which has been employed recently with success in other branches of archaeology where a sufficient number of examples is available: but we do well to remind ourselves that each brooch could prick the finger of its owner and that each had a very particular human association.

Brooches are occasionally seen on the garments represented in the later Anglo-Saxon manuscripts; round brooches fasten the cloaks or tunics of men on the shoulder or the chest, but women are but rarely depicted wearing a brooch, and there is no useful reference to jewellery in early literary sources. One or two general considerations must be remembered as we look at relics, the greater part of which have been recovered from burials. A woman or a man might be buried with all or only part of their treasures, with pieces which had a special family or folk significance or with broken jewels and ornaments of no real value which otherwise might have found their way to the melting pot or the rubbish pit. Ornaments may well have slipped from their original positions by the time the grave is opened by archaeologists, and some information recorded by early antiquaries may not always have been accurate enough though a few such as James Douglas took particular care that it should. There is sufficient evidence to show that the cloak or mantle was fastened in the usual classical way on the right shoulder, the position in which the finest jewelled brooches are generally found. Women's tunics were sometimes fastened by a brooch on each shoulder; pairs of brooches just below the shoulders and one below another on the breast were evidently to secure the fold-over of the tunic. Brooches were also used as we have already noticed to secure strings or festoons of beads. Long brooches were sometimes worn foot uppermost as the decoration seems to require, as a coin with a notable head was sometimes placed upside down in a pendant for better viewing by the wearer. As many as three long brooches have been found placed vertically on the lower part of the chest, and in one burial three large silver-gilt square-headed brooches were seen in their original position in a horizontal line on the ribs, the feet arranged to the left and right alternately.

The following account describes only main lines of development and the most interesting features of the leading varieties of brooches. Much more could be said, and readers who wish for further information on typology, chronology, and distribution both here and on the Continent should consult works listed in the Bibliography.

Saucer-brooches are of two types. The first, cast solid in one piece of bronze, has its geometric and zoomorphic pattern in Teutonic and semi-classical idiom, sharpened with a chasing tool and then silvered or gilded. The design was usually based on the manner of chip-carving in wood. Design and workmanship vary much in quality and execution. In the second type, the 'applied brooch', a thin bronze plate with an embossed and gilded or silvered geometric or zoomorphic pattern is cemented to a substantial disc of beaten bronze. There is sometimes a central bead of amber, garnet, glass, or occasionally of enamel, and in the latest of the saucer-brooches made after the middle of the sixth century there are wedge-shaped garnets to enliven the decoration. In the early brooches, some of them worn by the first invaders and adventurers, there are elements clearly derived from classical design, and many of the brooches of both types show features of their Rhenish descent. Occasionally, too, the human face appears in a much distorted form on saucer-brooches, and the full face is a constant feature of button-brooches, miniature jewels of cast and gilded bronze found in southern Britain and chiefly in the 'Jutish' regions.

Brooches of **annular** (ring) and **penannular** (broken ring) form derived from Celtic styles were commonly worn by Romano-British people. The Anglo-Saxon versions show a moulding or a faceting of the ring, sometimes with animal heads and even human masks in early examples. In Anglian districts a large flat variety soon won popularity but in general until the seventh or eighth centuries design was uninspired. But in the north of England, particularly in Northumbria (and in Ireland), by the latter part of the ninth century Viking influence had inspired jewellers to fashion large penannular brooches of silver with expanded and well-decorated terminals. Although strictly speaking it falls beyond the scope of the present book, there should be mentioned the most exciting of recent chance discoveries, that of three gold and silver brooches found with human bones on the island of Rousay in the Orkneys in 1963 by a man digging a hole to bury a dead cow. The finest, a massive cloak pin or penannular brooch of gold and silver decorated with bosses of amber can be dated by its style to about 750, and it is one of the outstanding Viking discoveries in Scotland during the present century.

The broad and handsome **quoit-form**, wide enough to receive a rich decoration of animal ornament, particularly heads of horses, human masks, all in carefully controlled zones, with very occasional patterns of foliage and plant tendrils, has been given much attention by specialists. Were these interesting silver brooches made by 'Jutish' craftsmen with southern Scandinavian traditions behind them working in the late fifth and early sixth centuries in the countryside centred around Canterbury, or did they come from northern Gaul where Roman traditions still survived in the jewellers' workshops? It is an interesting problem to which there is as yet no sure answer.

It is convenient to notice here the simple **disc-brooch**, a flat disc of bronze silvered or tinned to reproduce the appearance of silver and made more rarely of pewter. The decoration, punched or engraved or sometimes of open-work, is in geometrical patterns often based on interlocking circles which may be a native survival. In the ninth and tenth centuries there were disc-brooches of pewter cast in relief with prominent bosses and lentil-shaped patterns, and of bronze with clumsy backward-looking animals. A cast gilded bronze disc-brooch from Ixworth, Suffolk, now in the British Museum, bears an equal-armed cross with interlaced animal ornament in chip-carving in the field. This eighth-century brooch may well have been a poor descendant copy of the better-known Kentish circular brooches of an earlier period to which we shall refer shortly. A silver open-work disc-brooch of the tenth century from Cuxton, Kent, in the British Museum bears the inscription + AELFGIVVMEAH but the name *Aelfgifu* is no longer associated with the first wife of Aethelred the Unready (m. 1002) or the second wife of Canute (d. 1052). It is scarcely a royal piece, but it often attracts popular attention in view of its supposed owner's fame.

In recent years many people have been agreeably surprised to find that there is another kind of disc-brooch, large and elaborately decorated convex discs of silver and gold, which were worn in the Christian period. One found in 1958 by a gardener at The King's School, Canterbury – it was presented to the British Museum on the condition that it was known as The King's School, Canterbury, disc-brooch – is of silver engraved with degenerate interlace and animal patterns inlaid with niello and further decorated with small gold plates ornamented with scrolls of filigree and plant tendrils. Though unfortunately badly damaged it has been carefully treated in the Museum Research Laboratory as befits one of the most important pieces of tenth-century jewellery ever to be found in Britain, a link, it may be, with the Viking capture of Canterbury. Also in the British Museum are the ninth-century Strickland and Fuller brooches, the latter once thought to be a clever forgery but now proved to be genuine, and an eleventh-century brooch from Sutton in the Isle of Ely which had vanished since its first publication in 1705, until 1951 when the British Museum purchased it from a dealer in Dublin. The Strickland and Fuller brooches have been chosen for illustration here, but the Sutton brooch with its zones of complicated Ringerike zoomorphic ornament and on the back a long inscription partly in Roman characters and partly in cryptic runes, a rhyming curse of Christian times and then perhaps the owner's name with a prayer for protection, has a particular human appeal. It was

ploughed up in 1694 in a lead casket with silver coins of William
the Conqueror.

The most common types of brooch are conveniently classified
as **bow-brooches**. They are clearly related to Celtic Iron Age and
Roman 'safety-pin' brooches, but influences from Scandinavian
and eastern European sources also appear and local English
fashions are sometimes predominant. The **long-** or
cruciform-brooch is cast in bronze, usually with skill, and in the
wide range of its best varieties designed for popular appeal and
general use we can enjoy to the full the harmony between the art
and the craft of the Saxon jeweller. Essentially it consisted of an
arched bow with a foot of almost the same length which provided
at its back a catch-plate for a bilaterally coiled spring terminating
at the head in moulded knobs. The spring cover could be enlarged
into a distinct form of rectangular head-plate while the terminal
knobs of the spring became an integral part of the brooch,
although in early examples they were cast separately and notched
to fit a specially bevelled head-plate. The main English
development which perhaps took place after the main influence
from Scandinavia ceased before the middle of the sixth century
was towards an enlargement of the plane surfaces, the
incorporation of the knobs both plain and floriate, the provision
of side lappets below the bow, and sometimes in animal ornament
an extravagant exaggeration of the nostrils. Large flat surfaces
were cast with elaborate ornament though some small panels were
left plain and undecorated, the primitive knobs now giving place
to large flat adjuncts to the head-plate which sometimes show a
knowledge of the advantages of plastic form. These later stages of
development are almost wholly confined to Anglian territory.
The largest florid cruciform brooch ever found in Britain has a
length of 7·25 in. and exhibits very ordinary workmanship; it
came from a grave of a woman of distinction opened in 1875 in
the Castle Park, Longbridge, Warwick. Her other jewellery is
preserved with this ugly brooch in the British Museum. A variety
of the cruciform brooch, the so-called **small-long brooch** which
may be only two inches in length, is sometimes regarded as an
early sixth-century cheap imitation of the elaborate cruciform
brooches which can be more than six inches long.

The great **square-headed brooches** were in part contemporary with cruciform brooches. Some are of silver, others of bronze, and there is often a tendency towards a polychrome effect with chip-carved ornament, gilding, zigzag niellure, silver discs attached to the (usually) three rounded foot-terminals, and even by settings of garnet and enamel. Typologists recognize three main divisions and no less than sixteen sub-types. Early examples may have been brought to Kent by women from the Rhineland before the end of the fifth century. They were copied by jewellers in Kent for perhaps a century but the more elaborate examples lasted here and elsewhere well into the seventh century, still the ordinary jewels of peasant agriculturists.

Brooches with semicircular and **radiate-head-plate** and narrow-sided or expanded foot seem to be of Frankish or Jutish origin and where they are not trade imports they are few in number — it may be that they were copies of brooches worn in East Kent, probably in the sixth century. The most interesting, of silver gilt decorated with chip-carving, niello, and burnished garnets, one of a pair from Kent, has under the foot an inscription in runes difficult to interpret but perhaps naming its owner.

The few silver-gilt **equal-armed brooches** with chip-carving may well be direct imports from the Lower Elbe-Weser region in the early migration period. Their design is adapted from Roman or at least provincial-Roman forms.

Bird and animal brooches are small simple castings of bronze, sometimes enriched with garnet eye and tail. They may possibly commemorate some prowess or personal association, but they are far removed from the rich Romanian and Hungarian treasures which used to be claimed as their parentage.

Of other jewelled silver brooches, a unique **trefoil** with remarkable filigree work and cleverly set garnets is one of the most interesting in the British Museum collections. It was found in 1808 near Kirkoswald, Cumberland, with a large hoard of coins in a pottery vessel contained by the roots of a blown-down tree. The coins suggest an approximate date of 855.

The attractive **polychrome round brooches** with their garnet inlays are essentially products of the Kentish jewellers, but since comparative study of the Sutton Hoo treasure it has been shown beyond all reasonable doubt that they were made in the period between 550–600 and 700 and not earlier as was once thought.

Two main groups may be recognized. The first is a cast plate of silver or bronze, including isolated settings for garnets, wedge-shaped and T-shaped, zoomorphic decoration and serrated borders imitating filigree work all cast in one with the plate, and occasionally by niello decoration in relief. Some brooches bear secondary jewels set between the main garnets. The second group of rich and elaborate brooches of silver and gold have cloisons of some twenty various but relatively simple patterns compared with those of the Sutton Hoo jewellery, set with flat cut garnets often backed by gold foil to reflect light, green and blue glass, and the white shell-like material already noted. Usually the cloisons are grouped round a central boss, while decoration of gold wire filigree is applied on separate panels and as an outer edging. The magnificent composite two-plate gold brooches known from their Kentish find-spots as Kingston and Sarre II (or the Amherst brooch) are the most luxurious of their kind. The East Anglian jewellers represented at Sutton Hoo used much larger garnets and set them in cloisons of more complicated shapes, some of the cloisons being themselves covered with gold plates thus balancing the pattern of the very large flat-cut garnets.

Such jewellery with its fine swagger and often almost incredible technical accomplishment has a virtuosity which appeals to a modern public whose standards are those of a precision machine – so once claimed a very distinguished prehistorian. Of equal interest, surely, is its long descent from the Gothic cultures of the Black Sea and Romano-Celtic cultures represented in treasures from Romania, Hungary, Italy, Sweden, and the Low Countries.

Armlets and **bracelets** were not often worn with long-sleeved tunics falling at least to the wrists. Beads in simple strands were sometimes used, but in general the glass bangles, the simple penannular and twisted armlets of moulded bronze and spirals of silver strip could nearly all be legacies from Roman sources. An unusual piece is a silver bracelet from Faversham in the Gibbs Collection in the British Museum: its clever decoration incorporating a boar's head may denote a connection with Sweden.

In East Anglia, **wrist-clasps**, cuff-fastenings for leather or homespun tunics, of gilded bronze with geometric or zoomorphic decoration of taste and quality, must often have enlivened many a sombre garment.

Finger-rings. The ordinary woman's ring was of silver or bronze, either in wire, where the bezel consisted of a flattened coil, or a bead which was twisted back on the hoop to allow for expansion, or in a thin flattened strip coiled snakewise and with decorated terminals. In various forms they were in use over a very long period indeed, even well into Christian times. Finger-rings of bone from domestic animals, of iron and of ivory make an occasional appearance, and in the British Museum there is a handsome ring of deep red agate with a legend in runes, perhaps a magic formula, found somewhere in the west of England. There are gold rings decorated with animal masks, animals and interlace patterns dating in the ninth century, and a few very rare forms such as the River Nene ring in the British Museum with its two opposed decorated discs. These recall the gift-rings often mentioned in northern epic literature, and those with inscriptions have a particular appeal, especially when their owners or their donors can be identified and reasonable speculation made about their story, and when some proper attempt can be made to identify inscriptions in runes and Old English characters. And to finish this brief notice of finger-rings, we mention a remarkably fine example of gold set with an onyx intaglio with a *Bonus Eventus* and decorated with filigree scrolls and pellets from the Snape, Suffolk, ship-burial and made about 625, now in the British Museum, and two charming examples of gold in which enamel has been skilfully used, one from Canterbury or near, the other, with a central triangular cell of red enamel with circular cells of opaque white enamel at the angles, all set on a deep blue enamel ground, discovered somewhere in England, both now in the Victoria and Albert Museum.

Buckles and **clasps** and the **mordants** and **strap-mounts** which accompanied them were worn on the girdles by both men and women of all classes. They were common objects of everyday practical use and while the many varieties of form, especially that of the triangular or rectangular plate, encouraged the jeweller's decorative sense, ornament did not detract from essential purpose. To the archaeologist they can sometimes indicate relative chronology, tribal and trade fashions, and movements as reflected in patterns of geographical distribution, and they also present a brilliant aspect of discovery in the form of most luxurious and spectacular pieces of jewelled regalia. From the fifth- (or perhaps fourth-) century bronze buckles and counter-plates with chip-carving ornament in provincial Roman style it is a far cry to the richly ornamented gold and garnet-set buckle and clasps from the famous seventh-century barrow at Taplow, Buckinghamshire, and particularly to the royal regalia from the ship-burial at Sutton Hoo, but all gave opportunities to craftsmen of skill and now, in their way, form part of Everyman's heritage.

Girdle-hangers, or chatelaines, relics comparable with the Roman matron's keys, are usually of cast bronze with simple moulded or ring-and-dot ornament. The **silver-gilt spoons** usually accompanied by a **crystal ball** in a silver band-sling worn on the girdle by women in East Kent are also known in continental areas settled by the Franks. The spoons are often set with garnets and decorated with niello; the bowls are perforated, and their significance is a matter for speculation.

Swords of value for their age and personal associations are often mentioned in literature, and their mountings and hilts gave scope to the jeweller or more strictly perhaps to the metalworker. The grip and pommel may be decorated with silver wire or plates engraved with human, animal, and foliage ornament sometimes relieved with niello. A sword of the ninth century from Abingdon, Berkshire, (Ashmolean Museum, Oxford) with its fine hilt and a carved pommel in silver gilt of the same date found in Fetter Lane in the City of London (British Museum) are outstanding examples of their kind. The earlier harness of garnet-set sword mounts from Sutton Hoo, and the garnet-set gold pommel and gold filigree decorated mounts of the sword itself are even more outstanding in the application of the jeweller's art to a royal sword. Note should also be taken of the rings, either loose or solid, which were sometimes used to decorate the swords of high-ranking warriors. The matter of sword decoration cannot be discussed further here: the interested reader is referred to the authoritative works by Mrs H. R. Ellis Davidson and Miss Vera Evison listed in the Bibliography.

Two discoveries of Anglo-Saxon jewellery are of outstanding interest and of national importance: those from the Sutton Hoo boat burial and the Alfred Jewel.

SUTTON HOO

The pieces of magnificent gold jewellery were found by the excavators along the keel-line of the boat, nearer to the after wall of the collapsed wooden memorial chamber, with its weapons, ceremonial objects, and regalia, than to the forward wall against which had been placed the kitchen utensils, chains, tubs, and cauldrons. Details and a full discussion of these matters will be found in Dr R. L. S. Bruce-Mitford's British Museum *Handbook*, 1972 edition, listed in the Bibliography.

The jewellery chosen for illustration here is an enlarged detail of the purse lid with its graceful mounts, items from the sword and its harness, part of one of the pair of hinged shoulder-clasps, and the great gold buckle.

THE ALFRED JEWEL

A brief historical note will add to the interest of the jewel. Alfred (849–901) succeeded his father Ethelwulf, king of the West Saxons, in 871, at the age of twenty-two, and from the outset was in conflict with the Danes. After six years he was obliged to take refuge in the Isle of Athelney, but in 878 defeated his enemy in great force at Ethandun. Later the Danes invaded yet again and the rest of his reign was spent in fighting. He ruled for thirty years and was buried at Winchester.

6

Museums

The following is a hand-list of English museums which contain Anglo-Saxon jewellery and objects of allied interest. Intending visitors are advised to consult the current annual edition of *Museums and Galleries in Great Britain and Ireland* (ABC Travel Guides, Dunstable, Beds.) for details of addresses and opening times. Private collections and material from recent excavations undergoing study and treatment are not normally available to public view.

LONDON: The British Museum. The Victoria and Albert Museum. The London Museum, Kensington Palace. Guildhall Museum, Basinghall Street.

London Boroughs: Barnet, Herts. Gunnersbury Park, Ealing and Hounslow. Kingston-upon-Thames, Surrey.

Bedfordshire: Bedford. Luton.

Berkshire: Abingdon. Newbury. Reading.

Buckinghamshire: Aylesbury.

Cambridge: University Museum of Archaeology and Ethnology. Fitzwilliam Museum.

Cheshire: Chester.

Devon: Exeter.

Durham: Dormitory Museum, the Cathedral.

Essex: Colchester. Grays. Saffron Walden. Southend-on-Sea.

Gloucestershire: Bristol City Museum. Gloucester City Museum.

Hampshire: Southampton. Winchester, City Museum and Cathedral Treasury.

Hertfordshire: Hitchin. Letchworth. St Albans. Stevenage.

Huntingdonshire: Peterborough.

Kent: Canterbury. Dartford. Dover. Folkestone. Maidstone and Kent Archaeological Society Museum. Ospringe. Rochester.

Lancashire: Liverpool City Museums.

Leicestershire: Leicester. Market Harborough.

Lincolnshire: Scunthorpe. Lincoln.

Norfolk: Norwich.

Northamptonshire: Kettering. Northampton Central Museum.

Northumberland: Newcastle-on-Tyne, University Museum of Antiquities with Society of Antiquaries Museum.

Nottinghamshire: Newark-on-Trent. Nottingham City Museum.

Oxford: Ashmolean Museum. Pitt-Rivers Museum.

Rutland: Oakham School Museum. Rutland County Museum.

Somerset: Bath, Roman Museum. Shepton Mallet.

Staffordshire: Stoke-on-Trent, City Museum.

Suffolk: Bury St Edmunds. Ipswich.

Surrey: Croydon Public Library. Guildford and Surrey Archaeological Society Museum.

Sussex: Bexhill. Brighton. Chichester. Lewes and Sussex Archaeological Society Museum. Worthing.

Warwickshire: Birmingham City Museum. Nuneaton. Stratford-upon-Avon. Warwick County Museum.

Wiltshire: Devizes, Wiltshire Archaeological and Natural History Society Museum. Salisbury and South Wilts Museum.

Worcestershire: Evesham. Kidderminster. Worcester County Museum. Worcester City Museum.

Yorkshire: Hull. Leeds City Museum. Scarborough. Sheffield City Museum. York, Yorkshire Museum.

7
Select bibliography

Several of these books will enable interested readers to follow changes and differences of opinion on Anglo-Saxon jewellery and its archaeological, artistic, and historical significance. Many have full bibliographies. Some volumes of the relative *Victoria County History* contain interesting details of early discoveries and *Medieval Archaeology*, the journal of the Society for Medieval Archaeology, news of recent discoveries and views on current matters associated with the study of Anglo-Saxon jewellery. Colour slides of the jewellery are published by The Colour Centre, Farnham Royal, Slough, Bucks., and by Pictorial Colour Slides, 242 Langley Way, West Wickham, Kent.

Akerman, J. Y., *Remains of Pagan Saxondom* (London, 1885).

Baldwin Brown, G., *The Arts in Early England*, 6 vols (London, 1903–37).

Bateman, Thomas, *Vestiges of the Antiquities of Derbyshire* (London, 1848).

——— *Ten Years of Digging in Celtic, and Saxon Grave Hills . . . . Derbyshire, Staffordshire & Yorkshire* (London, 1861).

Blair, P. Hunter, *An Introduction to Anglo-Saxon England* (Cambridge, 1956).

Bruce-Mitford, R. L. S. 'The Snape boat-grave', *Proceedings of the Suffolk Institute of Archaeology*, **26**, part 1 (1952), 1–26.

——— 'Late Saxon disc-brooches' in Harden, D. B. (ed.), *Dark Age Britain: Studies presented to E. T. Leeds* (London, 1956).

——— 'The Pectoral cross', in Battiscombe, C. F. (ed.), *The Relics of Saint Cuthbert* (Durham, 1956).

——— *The Sutton Hoo Ship-Burial*, 2nd edn (British Museum, 1972).

Clarke, Joan R., and Hinton, David A., *The Alfred and Minster Lovell Jewels* (Oxford: Ashmolean Museum, 1971).

Clemoes, P. (ed.), *The Anglo-Saxons. Studies presented to Bruce Dickins* (Cambridge, 1959).

Collingwood, R. G., and Myres, J. N. L., *Roman Britain and the English Settlements* (Oxford, 1937).

Davidson, H. R. Ellis, *The Sword in Anglo-Saxon England* (Oxford, 1962).

Dolley, R. H. M. (ed.), *Anglo-Saxon Coins: Historical Studies presented to Sir Frank Stenton* (London, 1961).

Douglas, James, *Nenia Britannica* (London, 1793).

Evison, Vera I., 'The white material in Kentish brooches', *Antiquaries Journal*, **31** (1951), 197–200.

——— 'Early Anglo-Saxon inlaid metalwork', ibid. **35** (1955), 20–45.

—— 'Further Anglo-Saxon inlay', ibid. **38** (1958), 240–4.

—— *The Fifth-Century Invasions South of the Thames* (University of London, 1965).

—— 'The Dover ring-sword and other sword rings and beads', *Archaeologia*, **101** (1967), 63–118.

Faussett, Bryan (ed. C. Roach Smith), *Inventorium Sepulchrale* (London, 1856).

Harden, D. B. (ed.), *Dark Age Britain: Studies presented to E. T. Leeds* (London, 1956).

Hawkes, S. C. (ed.), 'Notes on Jutish art in Kent 450–575 (E. T. Leeds)', *Medieval Archaeology*, **1** (1957), 5.

—— 'The Jutish Style A. A study of Germanic animal art in southern England in the fifth century A.D.', *Archaeologia*, **98** (1961), 29–74.

—— *et al.*, 'The Finglesham Man', *Antiquity*, **39** (1965), 17–32.

Hodgkin, R. H., *A History of the Anglo-Saxons*, 2 vols, 3rd edn (Oxford, 1952).

Jessup, Ronald, *Anglo-Saxon Jewellery* (London, 1950; New York, 1953).

Kendrick, T. D. (Sir Thomas) *Anglo-Saxon Art to 900* (London, 1938; reprint forthcoming).

—— *Late Saxon and Viking Art* (London, 1949; reprint forthcoming).

Leeds, E. T., *The Archaeology of the Anglo-Saxon Settlements* (Oxford, 1913; reprinted 1970).

—— *Early Anglo-Saxon Art and Archaeology* (Oxford, 1936; reprinted 1968).

—— *A Corpus of Early Anglo-Saxon Great Square-Headed Brooches* (Oxford, 1949).

(See also under Hawkes, S.C. [1957], above.)

Moss, A. A., 'Niello', *Antiquaries Journal*, **33** (1953), 75–77.

Ordnance Survey, *Map of Britain in the Dark Ages*, 2nd edn (Chessington, Surrey, 1966).

Ozanne, Audrey, 'The Peak dwellers', *Medieval Archaeology*, **8** (1964), 15–52.

Philp, Brian (ed.), 'The Anglo-Saxon Cemetery at Polhill, Dunton Green, Kent', *Excavations in West Kent 1960–1970* (Dover, Kent Archaeological Rescue Unit, 1973), 164–214.

Rice, D. Talbot (ed.), *The Dark Ages* (London, 1965).

Speake, G., 'A seventh-century coin pendant from Bacton, Norfolk and its ornament', *Medieval Archaeology*, **14** (1970), 1–16.

Stenton, F. M. (Sir Frank), *Anglo-Saxon England* (Oxford, 1943).

Thomas, Charles, *Britain and Ireland in Early Christian Times A.D. 400–800* (London, 1971).

Wilson, D. M., 'A group of Anglo-Saxon amulet rings', in Clemoes, P. (ed.), *The Anglo-Saxons: Studies presented to Bruce Dickins* (Cambridge, 1959).

—— *The Anglo-Saxons* (London, 1960).

—— *Anglo-Saxon Ornamental Metalwork 700–1100*, British Museum Catalogue of Antiquities of the Later Saxon Period (London: British Museum, 1964).

8
Comparative dates

410	Honorius tells Britain to undertake its own defence
c. 449	Landing of Hengist and Horsa
c. 545	Narrative of Gildas
597	Aethilberht, King of Kent, converted by St Augustine
625	Death of Raedwald, King of East Anglia
627	Conversion of Edwin, King of Northumbria
642–55	Rule of Penda, King of Mercia
681–6	Conversion of South Saxons by Wilfrid
687	Death of St Cuthbert
735	Death of Bede
757–96	Rule of Offa, King of Mercia
793	Viking sack of Lindisfarne
850	Danes' first winter in England
870	Aethelred and Alfred defeat Danes at Ashdown
878	Alfred defeats Danes at Edington (Ethandun)
899	Death of Alfred
902–24	Edward the Elder reconquers South Daneland
919–54	Viking rule in York
973	Supremacy of King Edgar acknowledged at Chester
1016	Cnut accepted as King of England
1042	Edward the Confessor King of England
1066	Norman Conquest of England

9
List of plates

10
Notes on the plates

Plate 1 *(left to right)*

PINS OF SILVER, BRONZE AND BONE

1. Bronze pin with moulded knobs and triangular spangles attached to the head. It was worn on the left shoulder, and the play of light on the plates of polished bronze must have provided a brave show.
Length of pin 6·8 in.
Leagrave, Bedfordshire.

2. Small and delicate bronze hair-pin with pear-shaped amethyst bead at the head.
Length 3·8 in.
Cirencester, Gloucestershire.

3 *(above)*. Bone pin, probably for the hair, the flat head cruciform and with ring-and-dot pattern.
Length 2·7 in.
London.

3 *(below)*. Short and thick bone pin with truncated head and deep prominent groove below. Probably a hair-pin.
Length 2·5 in.
From the Thames in London.

4. Bone hair-pin, circular section, tapering throughout.
Length 4·2 in.
Milton-next-Sittingbourne, Kent.

5. Bronze pin with adjustable bronze wire ring in head.
Length 5 in.
Long Wittenham, Berkshire.

6 *(above)*. Bronze hair-pin, dull green patina, the head in the form of a cross, and head and the flat shank decorated on both sides with ring-and-dot pattern.
Length 4·3 in.
From a barrow on Breach Down, Kent.

6 *(below)* and 8. Pair of bronze pins with simple moulded terminals united by a bronze chain. From a barrow on Breach Down, Kent. It is far removed in design and execution from the luxurious gold and jewelled pin suites, and such small sets are usually thought to be hair ornaments.
Length of pins 2·2 in.; of chain 4 in.

7. Jewelled silver hair-pin with six garnets and filigree decoration on the flat head; two cells now empty may have contained shell.
Length 3·4 in.
Wingham, Kent.

All the above are in the British Museum.

1

Plate 2

GOLD PENDANTS

1. Pendant of reddish gold, clumsily made; irregular cloisons in a pattern which seems to result from an unskilful attempt to render the plait in cell-work. The cells contain sunken roughly cut thick garnets some of which lie on pricked gold foil. The biconoid loop with its filigree and exquisite plait is an integral part of the design. The deeply sunk gold medallion occupying the centre of the pendant is a barbarous copy of the *solidus* of the Emperors Mauricius and Theodosius (582–602) struck at Arles. Mr Speake has recently suggested that it is a clumsy product of the nearby Sutton Hoo workshops, and rightly emphasizes the zoomorphic creature formed by the five irregular cloisons below the loop.

Diameter 1·4 in. *British Museum.*

Found by chance in a mass of seaweed on the beach between Bacton and Mundesley, Norfolk, in the winter of 1845. *Seventh century.*

2. Neat and precise garnet *cloisonné* pendant of straw-coloured gold, the colour relieved by small pieces of light blue glass or paste in the cells of 'pitch-fork' form which range alternately. Level with the face of the pendant is included a gold *solidus* of Valentinian II (375–92), and by the damage done when the coin was inserted it is clear that the frame was not specially made for this particular coin. As two authorities have recently pointed out, the cloisons beneath the cleverly made cylindrical suspension loop form a zoomorphic double-headed creature. The pendant is a pertinent reminder that to the jeweller any roundel of gold, whatever its source, was an attractive medallion.

Diameter 1·2 in. *British Museum.* Forsbrook near Cheadle, North Staffordshire. *Seventh century.*

3. The Wilton (Norfolk) cross is one of the best-known of Saxon gold jewels. It is obviously by its form, that of a Greek cross, a Christian piece; its central feature is an original gold *solidus* of Heraclius I (610–41), the Byzantine Emperor who recovered the wood of the True Cross for the peoples of Christendom, and further, the coin is mounted so as to show, from the front, its reverse which bears a cross potent standing on a four-step base. It will be noted that the cross appears in the pendant upside down, while the effigy, hidden on the reverse side of the pendant, is in its proper position. The coin is held in the cross frame both on its obverse and reverse by beaded gold strips and there is, therefore, little doubt that the cross was not originally made to receive a coin of this size. The *cloisonné* has mushroom and step-pattern cells of the finest East Anglian workmanship; the gold work is quite substantial but its thickness is relieved by the surface-spread of the garnets which are set on foils well raised above the base of the cells.

The coin, it is clear, could not have been inserted in the frame before 610; the cross must have been made by a Christian jeweller though it is in a familiar pagan technique. It may well have come from the Sutton Hoo workshops.

Width across arms 1·8 in. *British Museum.*

Seventh century.

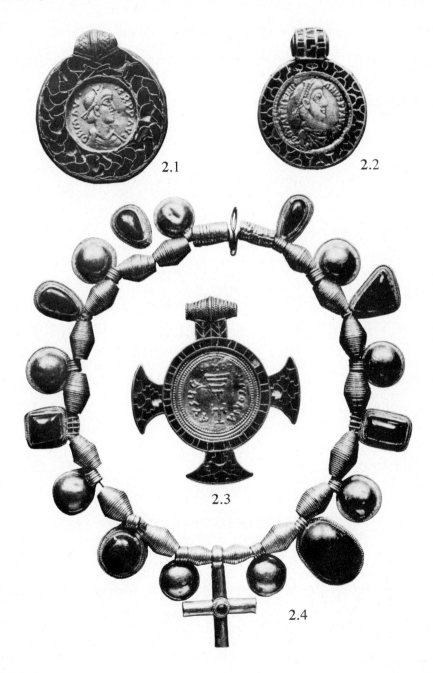

2.1

2.2

2.3

2.4

4. Gold necklace found in digging for iron ore about 1876 at Desborough near Market Harborough, Northamptonshire, near the head of a skeleton in a grave which, it is said, contained traces of fire; this and other graves were within an inconspicuous rectangular earthwork. The jewel consists of eight small cabochon garnets of circular, ovoid, rectangular, and triangular form, no two quite alike, nine circular beaded drops of plain gold, seventeen barrel-shaped beads of coiled gold wire, two similar cylindrical beads to house the clasp, and as its central feature a small pendant cross having a cabochon beaded garnet (originally on front and back) at the intersection.

Diameter of necklace about 3 in; barrel-shaped beads, length 0·4 in. *British Museum.*

Seventh century.

By permission of the Trustees of the British Museum.

Plate 3

1. THE IXWORTH CROSS

A famous gold pectoral cross with *cloisonné* garnet work was found with the detached top-plate of a gold filigree brooch in the Kentish or East Anglian style in a grave at Stanton, Ixworth, near Bury St Edmunds in West Suffolk.

There seem also to have been found in this accidental discovery the staples of a wood coffin, and it is worthy of note that the plate of the brooch was buried in its unfinished state with its owner.

The garnets in the Ixworth cross are mounted on foils sunk deeply into the prominent and precise cloisons. The top arm was broken at some time in antiquity when it was

repaired by solder and a brace, the dull red patina of which matches that of the rest of the cross. The bugle bead may belong to the time of the repair, for cells in the upper arm were distorted to receive it. It is a further example of the technique of a pagan Saxon jeweller used on a Christian ornament, and can be compared with St Cuthbert's Cross.

In the brooch, satellite bosses of shell were attached to the top-plate by slender pins, while the central boss, the collared aperture for which remains, was fastened to the back-plate.

Width across arms 1·5 in. *Ashmolean Museum, Oxford.*

Seventh century.

2. THE CANTERBURY CROSS

A cruciform brooch cast from light golden-coloured bronze found in St George's Street, Canterbury, in 1867 has been widely reproduced as 'The Canterbury Cross' and sold as a souvenir.

It is almost baroque in style. The decoration in shallow casting consists of a leaf- or vine-scroll, while to each arm with its curled terminals is attached a small triangular panel of silver incised with a nielled triquetra such as may be seen in the silver from the treasure deposited about 875 at Trewhiddle in Cornwall. A pin with a polygonal decorated head which retains traces of niello is closely similar to the Canterbury ornament, and the Trewhiddle style is a development in metal of a style familiar in southern English manuscripts.

The brooch now lacks its pin, but the support and catch remain, although there is some reason to

3.1

3.2

think that these were added later to the original cross. It is one of the small group of antiquities of the later Saxon period found in Canterbury, and it is not going beyond the bounds of possibility to suggest that they were lost in the Danish storming of the city in 851, the year in which according to the *Chronicle* '... the heathen now for the first time remained over winter in the Isle of Thanet'.

Width across arms 1·75 in. *Canterbury, Royal Museum.*

Ninth century.

Plate 4

ST CUTHBERT'S CROSS

Among the famous relics of St Cuthbert (d. 687) found at the opening of his coffin in 1827 was the jewelled cross, which by its deep burial in the folds of his robes, and secured by a golden cord, had escaped the savage desecration of the tomb at the time of the Dissolution. Together with the magnificent inscribed stole and maniple, embroidered by Queen Aelflaed of Wessex for Frithestan, Bishop of Winchester, and subsequently in 934 presented to St Cuthbert's shrine by King Athelstan, and the much-travelled wooden coffin incised with sacred figures, it forms one of the chief treasures of Durham Cathedral.

The cross is built up on a shaped plate of gold which has riveted at the junction of the arms a closed gold cell of conical form, bearing a sliced garnet resting on an exposed setting of shell derived from the Far East. There would be room in the cell for a very small relic. The arms of the cross have ranges of garnet-filled cloisons built up on a rectangular box-like structure of gold strip. The finely wrought decoration consists of a prominent serrated border, dummy rivets in collars, and beaded wire; the garnets are thick and not laid on foils as in characteristic Kentish works, but the jewel as a whole is of surprising thickness. The loop has a 'Kentish' style filigree decoration and may safely be reckoned as an addition to the original jewel.

There is evidence that the cross had been twice broken and repaired at some time in antiquity before its burial with the Saint. It was again broken at the time of its discovery in 1827; further repairs were removed in the British Museum Laboratory in 1936, and the cross was then carefully restored to its condition at the time of burial. The cross was probably of some age when it was buried. It exhibits certain Kentish or Anglian features and indeed a Celtic form, but it was almost certainly made by Northumbrian cloistered, and possibly old-fashioned, jewellers.

Width across arms 2·35 in. *Durham Cathedral, Dormitory Museum.*

c. 640–70.

Plate 5

BRACTEATES

These thin circular pendants of gold, embossed with human and zoomorphic designs, are among the most attractive relics of the Anglo-Saxon age. They have a loop for suspension and were normally worn as part of a woman's necklace. The design is a remote imitation of late Roman gold coins and medallions which circulated by way of subsidy to the barbarians in northern Europe far beyond the

4

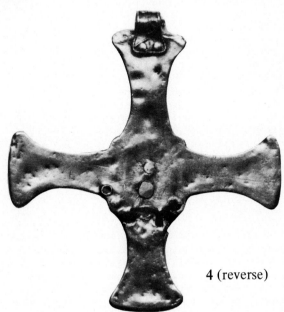

4 (reverse)

frontiers of the Empire. The decoration is stamped with a die, and more than one bracteate made by the same die is known. From their original home in Scandinavia, the bracteates arrived sometimes directly but more often indirectly in other Germanic lands, and there was an early contact between Denmark and England.

1, 2, 3. Three of four specimens from grave 29 at Bifrons, Kent, which with its radiate brooch and 'shield-on-tongue' buckle can be dated in the first half of the sixth century. No. 1 has a fantastic but carefully drawn human figure with raised arms, reminiscent of Late Roman coins, and strangely upturned legs, which is perhaps an attempt to represent a half forgotten version of Odin. Nos. 2 and 3 have a disintegrated interlace, and the decoration of the border of no. 2 is noteworthy.
Diameter of no. 2: 1·05 in.

4, 5, 6, 7, 8 are five of the six bracteates from the famous richly furnished Grave 4 in the Sarre cemetery, which can be dated just after the middle of the sixth century. Each bears a disintegrated ribbon-animal, carefully produced, and the wide border of no. 5 with its indents should be compared with the more usual border of pellets.
Diameter of no. 5: 1·25 in. *Kent Archaeological Society's Collection, Maidstone.*

9. From a woman's grave at Ash, near Sandwich, Kent. The edge and border are beaded; a schematic human face appears in the four arms of the cruciform pattern, and at the centre is a double loop in ribbon-work enriched with beading.
Diameter 1·2 in. *British Museum.*

10. From Market Overton, Rutland. The design is a very crude human figure, its head lacking, in a well-developed chip-carving technique which may result from the use of a wood die.
Diameter 1·2 in. *Ashmolean Museum, Oxford.*

11. One of a pair from a barrow at Wingham, Kent. The women buried had an urn at her feet; a necklace with beads, a cowrie-shell and the two bracteates; a silver bracelet and a fine garnet-set brooch; and the jewelled hair-pin illustrated in Plate 1, no. 7. The bracteates have tightly interlaced ribbon-animals, the bodies of which are emphasized by beading.
Diameter 1·1 in. *British Museum.*

Plate 6

SAUCER BROOCHES

1. A cast bronze saucer-brooch found on the left shoulder of a woman at Horton Kirby, Kent. An adaptation of a human face lies between the spiral-ended arms of a cross, and the wide surrounding border is of alternate vertical and horizontal hatching, the whole being cut in 'chip-carving' technique. The hatched border is an additional legacy from woodcraft, and the general atmosphere of the brooch with its powerful contrasts of light and shade set off by the narrow plain rim suggests that the maker was familiar with provincial Roman work. A Roman flagon was included in its owner's grave.

The moulds for these 'chip-carving' pieces have not

5.1

5.2

5.3

5.4

5.5

5.6

5.7

5.8

5.9

5.10

5.11

survived but there can be little doubt that some were of wood, and indeed the striations of wood-grain very occasionally appear in imperfectly finished castings. There would have been no difficulty in casting them in wax or clay, or in very fine moulding sand.

Diameter 1·9 in. *Kent Archaeological Society's Collection, Maidstone Museum.*

Fifth century.

2. One of a pair of bronze gilt applied saucer-brooches with deep flared rims having finely scalloped edges, and shallow plates roughly cast as they left the mould. The plates bear a cruciform motif, each arm being filled by a schematic human face and the intervening spaces by a disjointed animal leg with claws; the surrounding border is a much broken zoomorphic band. Fixed at the centre with a white cement of which traces remain, is a bead of deep blue translucent glass, an effective contrast to the gilding. The brooches were worn one on each shoulder.

Diameter 2·5 in. *University Museum of Archaeology and Ethnology, Cambridge.*

Barrington, Cambridge. *Sixth century.*

Plate 7

QUOIT-FORM BROOCH

This is a very beautiful and interesting brooch (it belongs to the annular or solid ring group) of punched silver, partly gilt, in which the detail has been emphasized by careful tracing. The pattern was beaten into the thin metal from the front of the disc. The pin is hinged and moves freely upon a sector of the inner ring, the point passing through a V-shaped notch in the side of the plate opposite and being secured on its return with the contained portion of cloth against one of two moulded studs. In use, the pin was pushed through the fabric of the dress which for this purpose was bunched into the central space of the brooch, the pin then being moved along its sector of the inner ring and the point secured against one of the stops by the pull of the cloth. Riveted to the hinge of the pin and to the plate, one on each side of the notch, are small dove-like birds cast in the round, one of the pair on the plate being on pivots; they have broad splayed tails, ringed necks, and the feathers are indicated by regular punch marks. The pairs of confronted animals on the outer band of ornament, and those of the inner band, pairs of confronted but frightened backward-looking creatures, may possibly be regarded as a representation of the familiar Roman subject of dog-and-hare. The indication of animal fur by lightly struck but incisive punch-marks is also a borrowing from Roman techniques. The inner ring may perhaps be an addition to the original form of the brooch.

Technically this brooch belongs to the earliest phase of the Germanic settlements and before the advent of the Germanic Style I animal ornament. The craftsman who made it could have come from southern Scandinavia or from northern Gaul with Frankish members of the ex-Roman army. Another view is that the craftsman was trained in Kent and moved subsequently to

6.1

6.2

7

Finland. Whatever its origin, the brooch is a fascinating study in its own right.

Diameter 3·05 in. *British Museum. Late fifth or early sixth century.* From Sarre or Crundale, Kent.

Plate 8

THE STRICKLAND DISC BROOCH

A splendid silver disc brooch with a convex surface decorated in an outstandingly bold design with inlaid gold and niello to emphasize the intense feeling of its carving. The centre is a dished cruciform figure with animal-mask terminals supported by a bold intricate quatrefoil field occupied by animal masks. A domed rivet with beaded wire collar is at the centre of the cruciform figure, with four others between the points of the quatrefoil field. The beaded outer border sets off two inner borders, one of pellets and lozenges, the other of inlaid gold. Around the bosses are decorations of inlaid gold plates bordered with lines of inlaid niello, and the animal masks are similarly treated. The animal eyes were originally of blue glass in cabochon, and altogether the brooch exhibits a very bold outstanding design. The back has fittings for the pin, which is not preserved, and there is a top suspension loop which appears to have been added later. In its form, technique, and most striking decoration, all of which are fully discussed in the books noted above, the Strickland brooch can be compared with the objects from the famous silver hoard of *c.* 875 found by tin-workers at Trewhiddle, St Austell, Cornwall in 1774 and now one of the treasures of the British Museum.

This brooch has no recorded find-spot, but was probably part of the collection of a well-known Yorkshire antiquary, Sir William Strickland (1753–1834). It was purchased by the British Museum in 1949 after an export licence was refused following its sale to an American collector. Its authenticity which had sometimes been held in doubt was fully confirmed by the British Museum Research Laboratory.

Diameter 4·3 in. *British Museum. Ninth century.*

Plate 9

THE FULLER DISC BROOCH

This fine silver disc brooch of no known provenance is also most skilfully engraved and decorated with niello inlay, but in contrast with the Strickland brooch it is a more delicate and elegant piece of work and is indeed one of the finest objects of its period known. Its design, in brief, is a central dished cruciform panel with a three-quarter length human figure thought to represent the sense of Sight. The curves of this panel bound four carvings of full-length human figures portraying the other four senses, Taste and Smell in the upper left and right areas, with Hearing and Feeling at the bottom left and right. Small domed rivets occupy the outer points of the central cruciform panel which is enclosed by a circle of billeted lines. The outer border consists of sixteen roundels bearing variations on designs of birds, distinctive floriated circles, backward looking animals, and the formally depicted head and shoulders of a human

8

9

figure. The whole background and engraving are filled with well-polished niello. The attachment pin at the back is missing though the seats for its rivets remain.

The brooch and its importance in Anglo-Saxon art and archaeology have been brilliantly discussed at length by Dr R. L. S. Bruce-Mitford who again calls attention to resemblances to the Trewhiddle hoard and to many other English and foreign related items of jewellery.

For many years the brooch was considered to be an ingenious fake, but detailed examination by the British Museum Research Laboratory proved its authenticity, and in 1953 Dr A. A. Moss had shown that its niello was of a type that was no longer used after the eleventh-century. It is named from its part-donor to the British Museum in 1952, Captain A. W. F. Fuller, to record his continuous faith in its authenticity when the brooch was discredited by all but one archaeologist, the late E. Thurlow Leeds.

Diameter 4·4 in. *British Museum. Ninth century.*

Plate 10
CRUCIFORM LONG BROOCH

Among Anglo-Saxon burials near the line of the Foss Way at Narborough Road, near Westcotes, Leicester, was one which yielded this well-made bronze cruciform brooch. It is of simple but pleasing over-all design with three ring-marked attached side knobs on the slightly concave top and sides of its head-plate which is decorated with a simple pattern in punched dots. This punched decoration appears also on the ridged bow and on the lobed foot which may preserve a memory of zoomorphic design in its shape. This well-cast and well-finished brooch is but one example of many hundreds in Britain.

Length 4·9 in. *Leicester Museums and Art Gallery.*

c. mid-sixth century.

Plate 11
FLORID CRUCIFORM BROOCH

This bronze brooch found at Stapleford Park, Saxby, Leicestershire, either in gravel-digging in 1827 or in laying the railway in 1890, in cemeteries with mixed cremation and inhumation burials is perhaps the most monstrous and fantastic piece of Anglo-Saxon jewellery known in Britain. The side knobs have lost their function and appearance. There are pieces of what might pass for chip-carving, the last wrecks of what were once animal forms filling up spaces which a skilled jeweller would have used to greater advantage. Whether it is truly a Mercian jewel or a piece from mid-Anglia must remain a matter of opinion, but if the former it might just possibly reflect the conservative background of Penda who ruled between 626 and 655 AD.

This is one of a small group of extremely florid brooches which will one day receive specialized attention.

Length 7·75 in. *Leicester Museums and Art Gallery.*

c. mid-seventh century.

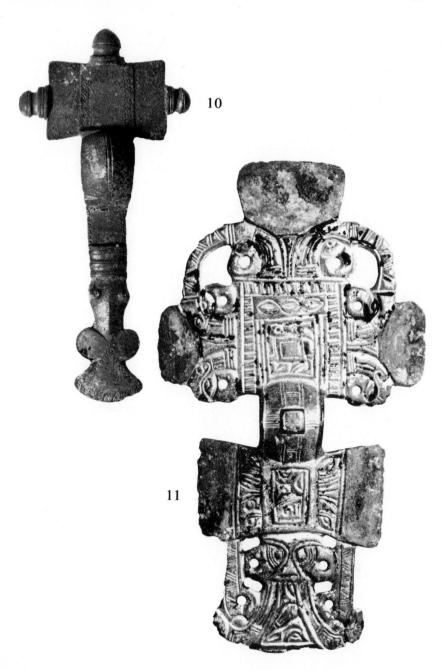

Plate 12

SQUARE-HEADED BROOCH

This is a characteristic example of the Anglian square-headed brooch in its developed form, a carefully finished one-piece casting in bronze, brightened with a graver and then gilded. The incurved head-plate has a complicated schematic animal pattern which appears also on the bow and the foot, while highly schematic human masks may be seen on the head-plate and again on each lobe of the foot. Altogether the brooch makes a fine display of light and shadow, and is of the kind which a leading archaeologist once described as 'glittering and winking like fireflies' in what he thought was the smoky gloom of filthy little Saxon dens. We now think rather differently about Saxon houses.

Length 5·6 in. *University Museum of Archaeology and Ethnology, Cambridge.*

Late sixth century. Barrington, Cambridge.

Plate 13

EQUAL-ARMED BROOCH

A cast silver-gilt brooch with crouching animals in a fully plastic chip-carving technique. Possibly it was secured by a catch-plate. It may be of continental origin or the product of an early British workshop.

Length 3·9 in. *University Museum of Archaeology and Ethnology, Cambridge.*

Fifth century. Haslingfield, Cambridge.

Plate 14

TREFOIL BROOCH

This trefoil silver filigree silver brooch was discovered near Kirkoswald, Cumberland, possibly in 1818, after a gale had blown down a tree, the roots of which had preserved a pottery vessel containing the brooch and six copper Northumbrian coins which can be dated about 855. It is a fine example of late Saxon ornamental jewellery, perhaps Viking plunder, which was already old when it was buried. The central and the one remaining terminal boss are encrusted with annulets bearing granules; part of a flat circular garnet may be seen in the terminal boss, a lingering memory of the far-off days of the polychrome *cloisonné* jewels. The main features of the decoration are the heavily serrated band filigree, the closely filled but not symmetrical vine-scroll, groups of fine granules, and the double-twisted wire and beaded edging. This interesting example of the silver-smith's work with hints of Scandinavian and Carolingian design and a prototype of certain Viking jewels of the ninth and tenth centuries has a long bibliography, English, Scandinavian and German.

Length 3·5 in. *British Museum.*
Eighth century.

Plate 15

CANTERBURY COIN BROOCH

This famous brooch, the largest of its kind, is made of twelve concentric rings of silver wire alternately beaded and twisted framing a central silver medallion, and is held together at the back by six clumsy splayed braces of silver strip with loop holdings for a catch. The obverse of the portrait medallion has a crowned head to the right with its mantle fastened by a

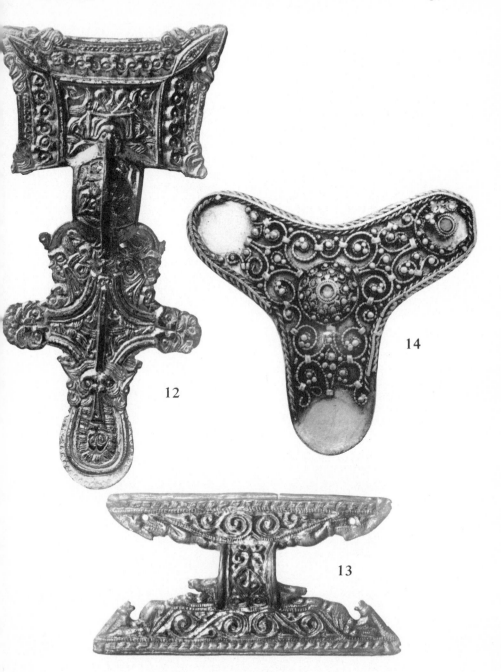

12

14

13

brooch under the chin or on the left shoulder and a legend easy to read as *Wudeman fecit* (WVDEMAN FECIÐ), while the reverse bears a small central cross and the legend NOMINE DOMINI. The style imitates that of the coinage of King Edgar (d. 975). A moneyer named Woodman worked at Shrewsbury under Edward the Confessor (d. 1066) but the name cannot have been uncommon.

The brooch was found many years ago at Canterbury perhaps in the River Stour, and this may not be unlikely on other grounds. It was purchased at the sale of Dr Harold Wacher, a well-known Kentish antiquary, in 1951 for E. Thurlow Leeds who then gave it to the Ashmolean Museum on condition that the donor was not named until after his death which took place in 1955. It has been most carefully cleaned and now has much of its original brightness; the reverse is clearly shown by a clever mirror-mounting.

Diameter 3 in.

Second half of tenth century.

Plate 16

POLYCHROME ROUND BROOCHES

These elaborate silver-gilt disc-brooches with finely set free-standing cloisons, gold filigree on a separate plate, and sometimes inlays of niello, are among the most attractive of the relics from the Saxon graves of Kent. Some fifty jewels of this style are known and nearly all reach a remarkably high standard of technical excellence. Their distribution shows that they were made at Faversham, which was the centre of a district noteworthy for its advanced political and economic development.

1. King's Field, Faversham, Deep red almandine garnets. The circular cells also held garnets, and the foils in one still remain. The polychrome effect is extended to the rim by the use of four rectangular garnet-set cells, niello annulets, and alternate lengths of plain metal and beading (light and shade) on the edge.

Diameter 1·9 in.

2. King's Field, Faversham. The apices of the triangular cells and the four inner step-sided cells contain blue glass.

Diameter 1·6 in. Both *British Museum.*

Early seventh century.

Plate 17

COMPOSITE 'KENTISH' BROOCH, SARRE I

From a woman's burial found accidentally in 1860. Other furniture in the grave included a large Coptic bronze bowl, which contained bones of sheep and ox, and an iron blade with a tang at each end, possibly a weaving batten symbolic of the woman's domestic background.

The thick, slightly concave, jewelled circular brooch of gold, now distorted but almost complete, lay on the left breast. The front and back plates are bound together by a gold strip with beaded edging, the interspace being filled with a white substance which is occasionally visible. The design is concentric about a sliced and bevelled garnet-crowned 'shell' boss held in an unusual serrated setting of gilded silver strip, with an inner and outer

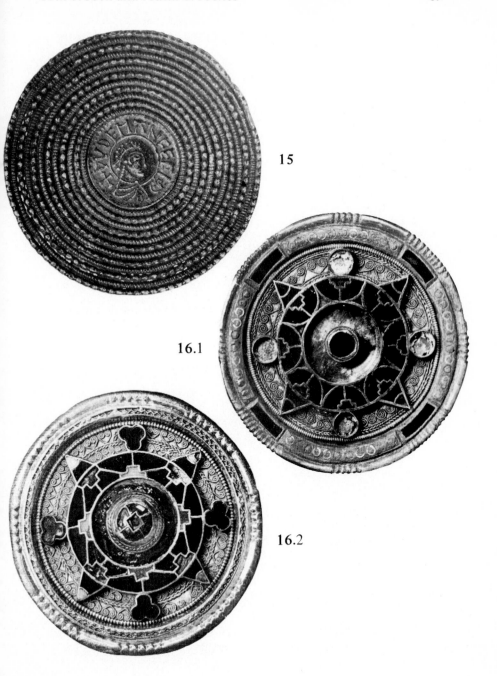

15

16.1

16.2

ring of garnet-filled cells separated by plate-units of gold wire filigree consisting of annulets and small tight scrolls. There are four satellite bosses of 'shell', each in a garnet-cell mount and having deep-coloured beaded cabochon garnets (one now missing) set on the crown. Each unit of filigree is complete in itself and stands on its own gold plate. It is awkward work: there are careless reversals of the scrolls, which vary considerably in size and tension, and the annulets are irregular in size and sometimes in number. The cloisons of the inner and outer rings are very regular in form but are badly planned and the spacing is bungled, although by simply reversing the sides of his cloisons the jeweller could have produced a comprehensive pattern of stepped cells alternating with wide honeycomb cells. Compare this brooch with, for instance, the brilliant and sparkling work at Sutton Hoo and on the Kingston brooch, and, on the other hand, with that of the careless Monkton brooch, Plate 19.

Diameter 2·6 in.

Included in the lady's necklace were four looped coin-pendants, all barbarous imitations of the gold *solidus*, from left to right of the Emperors Mauricius Tiberius (582–602), Heraclius (610–41), Mauricius, and of Lothair II, King of the Franks (613–28). An amethyst drop is at each end of the necklace in its present form, and there are fifteen annular beads and one rectangular bead of orange brown, green, red, and white opaque glass. At the centre is a flat gold-bound circular pendant, 0·95 in. in diameter, filled with a glass mosaic of minute light blue and white squares contained within a bold red chequer. Such work is Roman in its technique, and the pendant was perhaps made in Gaul by Romano-Gallic glass workers from a mosaic imported in bulk from Egypt, or possibly in the Roman glass works of the Rhineland.

The coin-pendants point to an approximate date for the necklace which must have been worn early in the reign of Heraclius; there is all the difficulty of dealing with the evidence of barbarous coin copies, and the mosaic glass pendant is certainly an antique, but the burial seems likely to have taken place between, say 620 and 650.

British Museum.

Plate 18
COMPOSITE 'KENTISH' BROOCH, SARRE II

This fine jewelled brooch, known as the Amherst brooch or Sarre II to distinguish it from the British Museum brooch illustrated in Plate 17, was found many years ago in a grave uncovered accidentally by gravel-diggers and had with it a handled bowl of Coptic form. The case of the brooch with its carefully made step, triangular, and quatrefoil cloisons, is of gold, while the back plate, decorated only by a single garnet on the head of the pin-housing, is of silver. When its then owner, Lord Amherst, accidentally dropped the brooch at a meeting of the Kent Archaeological Society in 1859, it was seen to be filled with a 'white substance'. The subsequent repairs are clearly visible. Though it is an elegant and beautiful jewel, this brooch shows some falling off in design and technique when compared with the Kingston brooch

though it is a far more carefully constructed piece than the Monkton jewel illustrated in Plate 19. Green glass fills the eight triangular cells. The gold foils underlying the garnets are boldly chequered with large and small rectangles made by a metal die. Again, the quality of the filigree work in the eight units of the Amherst brooch is both uncertain and bungled. Evidently apprentice hands were sometimes allowed to undertake important work in the Kentish workshops, occasionally with indifferent success if the Kingston brooch is taken as the masterpiece standard.

Diameter 2·2 in. *Ashmolean Museum, Oxford.*

Early seventh century.

Plate 19

THE MONKTON 'KENTISH' BROOCH

This most unusual example of a Kentish garnet-set gold brooch was found in one of a group of twenty-two Anglo-Saxon graves uncovered at Monkton, Kent, in 1971 during excavations for the Thanet section of the North Sea gas pipeline. The site is barely two miles from Sarre, the source of two of the finest of the Kentish jewelled brooches: indeed its careless execution can be compared in certain features with the Sarre brooch found with the coin-necklace. The brooch is of the most unhandy and careless journeyman workmanship, but clearly influenced by the styles of Kingston, Dover, and Sarre: much of the material is reused. The silver back-plate exhibits the outline engraved pattern of a *cloisonné* brooch with some faults in design

and execution, and it has been reused from a slightly larger brooch which had the elaborate type of pin-mounting and catch-plate of the Kingston and some other jewelled brooches. On the front, the cloisons of the inner ring include clumsy arrangements of two different types of cell-work, and the walls of the cells are of bronze and not of the usual gold. The gold of the brooch is very pale in colour and as Mr P. D. C. Brown kindly tells me, analysis shows it to be of about 50 per cent in purity in the rim and only about 40 per cent in the binding of the central boss. The gold filigree is poor in design and again very unhandy in execution. The whole brooch is in fact a ham-fisted remake, and one would like to know much more about the circumstances of the woman with whom it was buried, accompanied by a necklace of amethyst and polychrome beads. Was she related to an apprentice jeweller whose work she loved, or did the material which may have had some special social or folk significance find its way out of the Sarre workshop piece by piece? Whatever one may guess, this is one of the most human of problems ever set by a piece of Kentish jewellery.

Diameter 4·9 in. *Ashmolean Museum, Oxford.*

Purchased with the aid of grants from the Friends of the Ashmolean and the National Art-Collections Fund, 1972. *Six to seventh century,* rather later than the Sarre brooch.

Plate 20

THE KINGSTON BROOCH

This beautiful composite brooch consists of two plates of gold bound

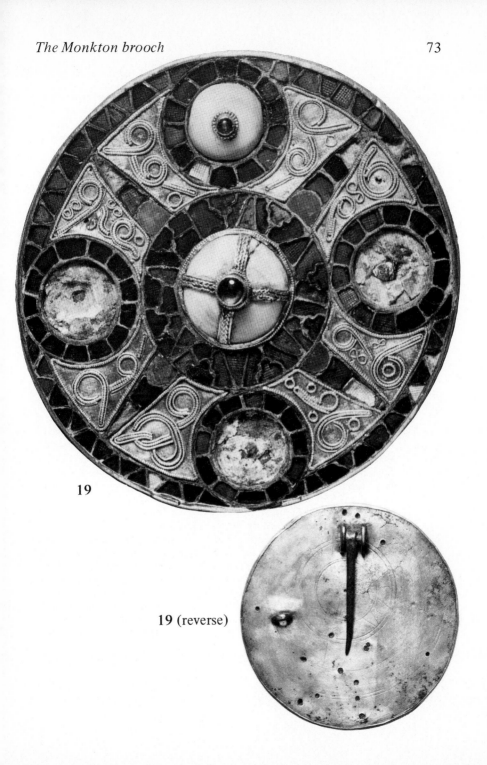

19

19 (reverse)

together by a strip of beaded gold wire filigree 0·25 in. wide, the interior being filled with a white clay-like substance, and the whole secured by three small clasps of gold set close together across the filigree on the rim.

The front plate is slightly convex, so that the concentric pattern of the face does not lose its perspective and individuality in the obscurity of a plane surface: the design is further controlled by its modified cruciform pattern as well as by the prominent central boss. There are five concentric rings of gold cloisons – among them step-shaped, square, semicircular, and tri-angular – each cell being very skilfully soldered to the front plate and to its neighbours at their points of contact. What would otherwise be a uniform carpet-like spread of garnet and gold is relieved by cleverly spaced triangular and step-shaped cells of blue glass; by four (one is now missing) square cells of a deeper red garnet; and by a central and four satellite bosses containing a white shell-like material which originally had a waxy surface.

On the back, the animal-head catch-plate for the bronze pin and the drum-like head of the pin and its surround are enriched with gold wire filigree; the head of the pin is jewelled with garnets, and above it is a safety loop for securing the brooch to the dress.

The cloisons and the units of filigree work are finely prescribed, the latter consisting of fine-beaded gold wire soldered to a prepared ground of gold on which the outline of the pattern had already been raised. The twisted knot and interlace pattern was a bold translation into filigree of the familiar Teutonic backward-biting quadruped. The brilliance of this fascinating mosaic of garnet set on gold foils, of blue glass, shell, and of gold filigree is exact and precise in its execution.

The Kingston brooch is the most noteworthy piece of the rich jewellery of Kent, a mark of the period of wealth and political ascendancy of the Jutes under Aethilberht in the seventh century, when a jeweller was able to spend more than a year in the peaceful surroundings necessary for the creation of such a treasure.

Something is known of the woman who owned this brooch. She was wealthy, and scarcely handsome. Her imposing belongings in the grave consisted of two remarkable unilateral-spring brooches of silver associated with a chatelaine at the waist, a gold pendant with *repoussé* decoration, a biconical pottery beaker, a cup of green glass, and two bronze-handled bowls with their trivet-stand. The bones of a child, probably from an earlier burial on the site, had been collected in a heap outside her coffin at the foot. The brooches with unilateral springs are excessively rare in a Saxon context. The Kingston pair seem almost certainly of La Tène type, and there may be some possibility that they were buried with an Early Iron Age child whose grave was disturbed by the construction of the Saxon barrow. Saxon veneration for the graves of antiquity is not at all uncommon.

Diameter 3·3 in. Weight 6·25oz.
City of Liverpool Museums.
Seventh century.

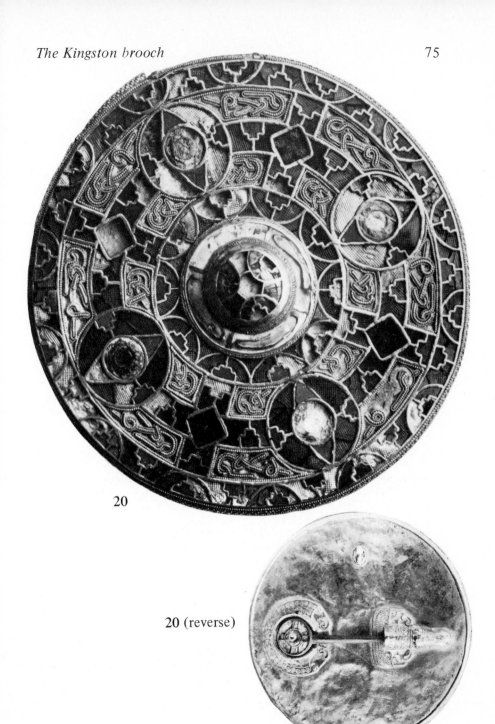

20

20 (reverse)

Plate 21

TWO MERCIAN JEWELS

These two pieces have had an interesting history since they were discovered about 1767 in White Lowe (Mander's Barrow), an earthen barrow, one among a group of stone barrows, on Winster Common, Derbyshire, which was being levelled under the power of the Enclosure Acts. According to an account read to the Society of Antiquaries on 17 March 1768 the barrow contained two globular green glass bottles, a silver collar or bracelet 'joining at the ends in dovetail fashion and studded with human heads', the circular brooch here illustrated, glass and 'earthen' beads, and the remains of a small bronze-bound wooden box in which the treasures had been deposited. By 1848 when Thomas Bateman wrote his book *Vestiges* only the circular brooch was thought to have survived and it belonged to the landowner, John Mander. After passing through the hands of three collectors, it was acquired by Bateman; but this was not all, for Bateman had already bought a small gold pendant cross which had been purchased from the labourer who found it about 1767 and had been in the successive possession of several other collectors. It is highly probable, says Bateman, that it was found with the circular brooch with which, he adds, it is almost identical in style.

1. This silver-gilt round brooch has a well-fitted silver back-plate, but no attachment pin remains. The large central boss, probably of garnet but long since missing, is encircled by a round of *cloisonné* garnets originally set on hatched gold foil, four step-shaped cells arranged in a cruciform pattern, separated by four pairs of unusual petal-shaped cells. There is then a circle of loose interlace filigree and an outer zone of tight S-shaped filigree with a beaded border. Four circular garnet bosses in beaded collars again in cruciform pattern, lie between the two zones. The style in general follows that of the familiar garnet-encrusted Kentish jewellery, but is less precise in design and execution. Somewhat similar but much finer petal-shaped garnets appear also on the bosses of the Sutton Hoo sword-scabbard, but they do not seem to be known elsewhere.

2. The small equal-armed pendant gold cross has a central faceted garnet boss secured by a beaded mount, double rows of scroll-pattern filigree on the arms and a border of beaded gold wire. At the base of the plain lateral suspension loop is a line of plaited filigree. This fine little jewel like those from Wilton, Stanton, Ixworth, and St Cuthbert's cross illustrated in this book is certainly a Christian emblem. Except for Wilton, however, it is the only example decorated with filigree, though filigree is often used on the equal-armed crosses which are marked features of disc-pendants.

Like the Kentish and East Anglian jewellers, the Mercian craftsmen had their own workshops in which local variations of style were produced. The custom of burying valuable pieces in bronze-bound wooden boxes was followed in each of these regions.

Diameter 2·6 in. Length 1·8 in.
Sheffield City Museums. Bateman Collection.

Mid-seventh century.

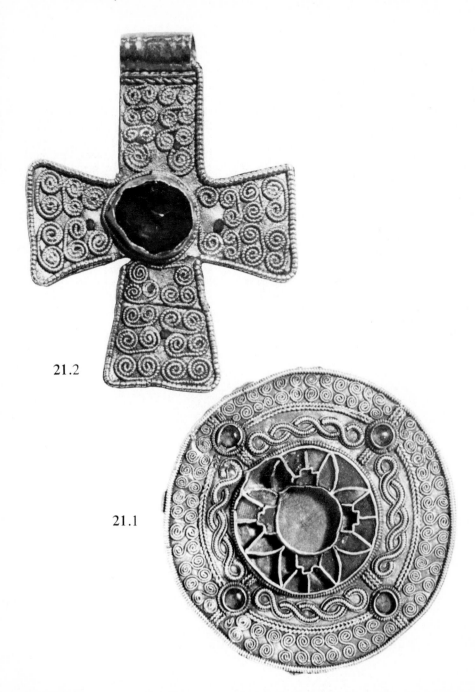

21.2

21.1

Plate 22

WRIST CLASPS

A pair of finely gilded bronze sleeve-ornaments for fastening the leather cuff of the tunic, found in 1880 at Barrington, Cambridge.

They were associated with applied saucer brooches, an iron key, bronze, ivory and iron rings, probably the frame of a purse, and a skein of twenty-nine flat red amber beads and one spherical crystal bead; the woman seems to have died in the latter part of the sixth century. The casting is skilled, and brightened by a fine graver before gilding; there are holes for sewing the clasps to the tunic, and it will be noticed that the left-hand side of each clasp is cast in one piece with the triangular extension, while the right-hand side fastens with a flat hook.

In the elaborate zoomorphic ornament can be distinguished the eye and limbs of the 'helmet-and-head' element, but it is their own version of the pattern which is presented by the Anglian school of jewellers.

Length 3·4 in. *University Museum of Archaeology and Ethnology, Cambridge.*

Late sixth century.

Plate 23

BRACELETS AND RINGS

1. Finger-ring of one piece of silver wire, coiled bezel.

Diameter 0·9 in., so probably a thumb-ring. *Collection of the Kent Archaeological Society, Maidstone.*

From the richly furnished *mid-sixth-century* Grave 4, Sarre, Kent, cemetery, 1862.

2. Finger-ring of bone, well finished and ornamented with a deeply cut cross pattern.

Diameter 1 in., probably worn on the thumb. *Gravesend Public Library.*

From a cemetery at Northfleet, Kent, which included cremation burials and early brooches.

3. Bronze bracelet of circular section, very much worn at one place, no doubt in the performance of its owner's domestic duties. It was worn by its last owner on the upper part of the right arm.

Diameter 2·9 in. *Ashmolean Museum, Oxford.*

Fairford, Oxfordshire.

4. Bracelet of transparent light-green moulded glass, much pitted, worn on left fore-arm.

Diameter 3·7 in. *Ashmolean Museum, Oxford.*

Chatham Lines, Kent, 1780.

5. Spiral ring, a flat silver strip of three coils and blunt terminal ornamented with dots and rings, worn on the third finger of the left hand. The type was worn in the Early Iron Age.

Diameter 0·7 in. *Ashmolean Museum, Oxford.*

Purwell Farm, Cassington, Oxfordshire.

Plate 24

FINGER-RINGS

1. Ethelwulf's ring

A very fine massive ring of dull reddish gold with splendid niello enrichment on the reserved metal. Found by chance in 1780 in a field at Laverstoke in the valley of the Upper Test 'prest out of a cart-rut sideways'; the present crushed and battered condition of the ring

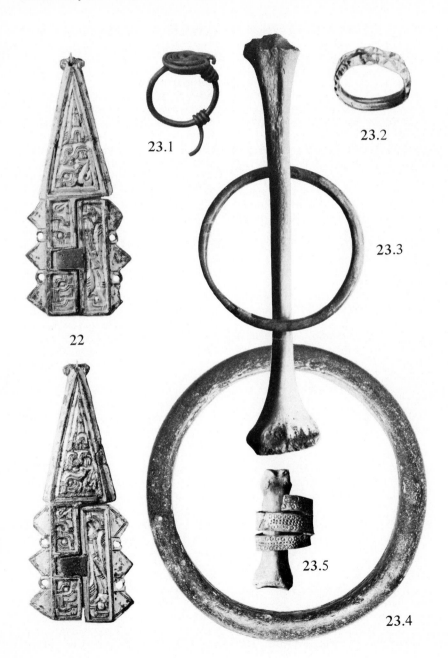

23.1

23.2

22

23.3

23.5

23.4

reflects the circumstances in which it was found, but it exhibits in addition signs of considerable normal wear.

It has a flat hoop beaded on the lower edge, the upper edge being defined by a very narrow plain margin. The mitre-shaped bezel bears a familiar motif, a conventional sacred tree with a bird, perhaps a peacock, facing it on each side, all reserved in the gold and finely set off against the niello ground. The sacred tree and birds are well known in Oriental art and in early Christian contexts, but here the birds are grotesque and executed with a clumsy barbarism which is also a feature of the foliage in plain relief at the angles of the bezel and of the loosely interlaced ivy-leaf terminal, quatrefoil foliage, and the encircled rosette, all enriched with niello, on the back of the hoop. The intricate detail is rigidly confined by its small panels. The two roundels on the tree are left free of niello and balance the two pieces of notched leaf plain foliage. Most of the niello, which was fused with great skill to a ground deeply roughened for the purpose, still remains.

The legend, also enriched with niello, reads + ETHELVVLF REX, and its attribution to Ethelwulf of Wessex (839–58), father of Alfred the Great, is undoubtedly correct. If it were lost in one of the many struggles with the Danes in the early years of Ethelwulf's reign, that in 840 at Southampton would on geographical grounds perhaps be the most likely.

(It should be noted here that rings inscribed with a personal name may have been the owner's property or a gift made by the owner.)

Diameter 1·04 in. Weight 285

grains. *British Museum.*

2. Ethelswith's ring

Two pieces of jewellery belonging to members of Ethelwulf's family have been preserved, the famous Jewel associated with Alfred, his youngest and favourite son, and an interesting finger-ring inscribed with the name of his daughter Ethelswith who, in 853, married Burhred, King of Mercia. There was, it seems, a considerable difference between the ages of the two children, and Alfred was but four years old when his sister was married.

Ethelswith's ring was found in 1870 between Aberford and Sherburn, in the West Riding of Yorkshire, by a ploughman who pulled it from the ground on the tip of his coulter, and so little was it valued that the finder attached it as an ornament to the collar of his farm-dog. A York jeweller subsequently exchanged it for tablespoons, and the ring passed by way of Canon Greenwell, the noted barrow-explorer of his day, to Sir Wollaston Franks and thence in the munificent Franks Bequest to the British Museum.

This richly decorated and heavy ring of finely burnished deep yellow gold has a slightly bevelled plain hoop enlarged on the pearled shoulders to meet a bold circular bezel with a pearled border. Each shoulder is ornamented with a small fanciful monster, possibly a boar, squatting on its haunches, while the central medallion of the bezel contains within a quatrefoil enriched with very degenerate palmettes the Agnus Dei between the letters A and

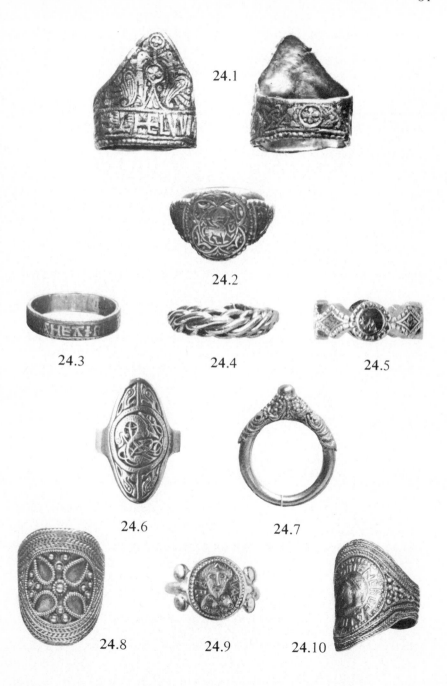

24.1

24.2

24.3

24.4

24.5

24.6

24.7

24.8

24.9

24.10

D (for the Greek words 'Lamb of God'), the latter appearing as the 'thorn' rune. The decoration is chased by an exceedingly competent hand, and enriched skilfully by niellure.

The inner side of the bezel has a sharply engraved legend which contrasts strongly with the worn condition of the ring. It may be read + EATHELSWITH REGINA, and it has been suggested that it was so marked to record a gift made by the Queen to a Yorkshire shrine. Ethelswith died in 888 on a pilgrimage to Rome and was buried at Pavia.

Diameter 1·02 in. Weight 313 grains. *British Museum.*

3. Aedred's Ring

A substantially made uniform hoop of reddish gold with a flat pearled edge showing signs of wear. Found in Lancashire, but details not known.

The interest lies in the legend reserved in the gold on a ground of niello, which employs both a normal Saxon form of lettering and runes. It may be read: + AEDRED MEC AH EANRED MEC AGROF: 'Aedred owns me: Eanred engraved me.'

Diameter 0·92 in. Weight 113 grains. *British Museum.*
Ninth century.

4. A Viking Period ring

Gold ring of stout plaited wire, the hoop beaten flat at the back. No locality.

Victoria and Albert Museum, Waterton Collection.

Other notable examples in gold in this style are the three plaited wire rings from Hamsey Churchyard, Sussex, and two rings from Soberton, Hampshire, all of which are in the British Museum.

5. Alhstan's ring

This ring was found about 1773 by a labourer on a common at Llys Faen between Colwyn Bay and Abergele, in Denbighshire. It was once worn on the necktie of the finder.

It is a thick and heavy hoop of rectangular section, the interior roughly finished, having alternately four circular and four lozenge-shaped panels, bordered with rectangular notches. The decoration is chased and relieved with niello, most of which remains. That in the lozenge-shaped panels is a schematic animal broken to fit the panel, a degenerate version of the long-snouted open-mouthed monster of ribbon-style whose characteristic head and eye is still recognizable. The letters ALHSTAN which appear in the four circular panels, suggest identification with Ealhstan, Bishop of the great diocese of Sherborne (817–67).

This warrior-prelate led the campaign which in 825 secured Kent for the kingdom of Wessex; in 845 he battled with the Danes at the mouth of the Parret, and it may be that he accompanied Ethelwulf's expedition when in 853 the united forces of Wessex and Mercia proceeded against the men of North Wales. In such a way could his ring have come to Llys Faen (Lysfaen).

Diameter 1·2 in. Thickness 0·15 in. *Victoria and Albert Museum. Ninth century.*

6. The Chelsea ring

Ring of silver gilt, plain hoop expanded into a large and curved oval bezel. The central circular panel of the bezel is completely filled by a grotesque animal with interlaced limbs and tail, the body and the border of the panel being emphasized by minute rectangular punch marks. The four remaining panels of the bezel have degenerate foliage with thickened terminals.

Length of bezel 1·3 in. *Victoria and Albert Museum.*

From the Thames at Chelsea, 1856. *Late eighth or early ninth century.*

7. Meaux Abbey ring

A fine gold ring dug up in the Moat at Meaux Abbey near Beverley, East Riding of Yorkshire, about 1867. It has a plain hoop of circular section, the shoulders of which are heavily encrusted with beaded wire filigree supporting a granular setting for the bezel, a small and plain sphere of gold. The decoration is in the form of animal, possibly boars', heads, and should be compared with that on the Alfred Jewel and on Ethelswith's ring.

Diameter 1·05 in. Weight 282 grains. *Victoria and Albert Museum.*

Ninth, or possibly early tenth, century.

8. Garrick Street ring

A medium-weight ring of pale yellow gold, found in Garrick Street, off St Martin's Lane, West Central London, but no particulars of its discovery survive.

It has a very large and curved oval bezel, the broad outer margin of which is built up of chevron-twisted gold wire flattened by the use of a draw-plate. The broken texture, with its contrast of light and shade, well sets off the open central field with its petal-shaped loops of beaded wire laid clumsily in a loose cross-pattern, and completed by a series of plain gold pellets set in small rings of beaded wire.

The cross-pattern may be a Christian symbol.

Diameter 0·9 in. Weight 185 grains. *British Museum.*

Ninth century.

9. Avfret's ring

A well-burnished ring of light-coloured gold. Four pellets on the plain hoop support a circular signet bezel which bears a boldly cut moustached and bearded man's head with ring-and-dot pattern, possibly dress ornaments, below. In the field on each side of the figure is cut the legend + AVFRET, the letter R encroaching slightly on the beard of the figure. Found about 1859 in Rome with a considerable number of coins of Alfred the Great.

If the famous and much disputed passage in the Anglo-Saxon *Chronicle* which described the sending of alms to India can be accepted as genuine, we need possibly look no further for an explanation of the presence of Avfret's ring and Alfred's coins in Rome: 'and that same year [under 883] led Sighelm and Athelstan to Rome the alms which King Alfred ordered thither . . . '

Diameter of bezel 0·65 in. *Victoria and Albert Museum.*

Ninth or tenth century.

10. Ehlla's ring

This fine but light-weight ring of pale yellow gold was found in a meadow at Bosington near

Stockbridge, Hampshire, by a labourer who saw its glitter in a pile of peat. The tall oval bezel is built up of chevron-twisted and flat-drawn wire opened out from the hoop which on each shoulder bears thirteen plain globules of gold. The bezel contains a central medallion, of darker metal but of one structure with the body of the ring, bearing the head of an ecclesiastic to right, and in the margin the legend: NOMEN EHLLA FIDES IN XPO: *'My name is Ella, my faith is in Christ'*. Nothing is known of the owner, but from its style the ring may be dated in the seventh century.

Height of bezel 1·5 in. *Ashmolean Museum, Oxford.*

Plate 25

BELT BUCKLES

1. A fine gold and garnet buckle from the burial of the rich seventh-century chieftain at Taplow, whose name, Taeppa, is retained in the place-name of this Buckinghamshire town. It fastened his gold embroidered cloak on the left shoulder. The flat and wide-hinged ring had sliced garnets and two pieces of blue glass, the tongue six garnets, each upper boss one, and the lower boss a central quatrefoil garnet surrounded by eight sliced garnets, all of which are in thick coarse cloisons. The interlaced filigree ornament is an excellent example of the Ribbon Style based ultimately on Romano-Germanic ornament which may have originated in Scandinavia or in Italy. Here it exhibits a kind of chip-carving style and is bounded by gold wire drawn to simulate beading.

Length 4 in. *British Museum.*
Seventh century.

2. This remarkable iron buckle plated with silver and with silver inlaid loops has a clumsy decoration in low *repoussé* depicting the bust of a man with uplifted hands, flanked on each side by a leaping lion, surmounted by a peacock and trampling on a lamb. The outer border of the plate – that on the counter-plate is lost – bears the legend: VIVAT Q . . . VI FECIT: 'Long live the man who made [me]'. The design of Daniel in the Den of Lions and other features suggest that the buckle was made in a North Gaulish workshop, and it must have come to Britain on the belt of one of the earliest invaders. It was dug up by a gamekeeper at Bifrons, Kent, in 1867 and after treatment with glue was sewn to a card for preservation by the gamekeeper's daughter.

Length 3·6 in. *Kent Archaeological Society's Collection, Maidstone Museum.*
Fifth century.

Plate 26

THE 'FINGLESHAM MAN' BUCKLE

This remarkable gilt bronze buckle was found in 1964 during the excavation of a previously known Anglo-Saxon cemetery at Finglesham near Deal in east Kent. In view of its outstanding interest it has been published in advance of her full excavation report by Mrs Sonia Chadwick Hawkes, and there is no doubt that its bibliography will increase steadily. It will certainly occupy the attention of many students of Anglo-Saxon and Germanic art and archaeology and, as Mrs Hawkes and her fellow-authors emphasize, those of Germanic religion and mythology in addition. The buckle lay at the waist of a man

25.1

25.2

whose body was buried with two sets of shoe buckles and lace tags, a spear, knife, a wooden box and a bucket, and a red pottery bottle. He was scarcely a man of great wealth but had some standing and importance.

On the buckle the chief feature of interest is the figure of a horned man cast in low relief. His helmet bears horns terminating in beaks, he carries a spear in each hand and wears nothing but a broad buckled belt. Who is this almost naked man with bold staring eyes and severe pointed chin, three-fingered hands, and bent knees? He seems to belong to the early traditional symbolic heathen religious art, versions of which were current in northern Germany and Sweden in the seventh century, a version it may be of the very ancient but well-attested Horned God. The form of the buckle is Kentish enough: perhaps its maker copied his man from a Swedish helmet he had seen in Kent.

Length 3·1 in. *Private collection. Mid or second half of the seventh century.*

Plate 27

BUCKLE OF QUOIT-BROOCH STYLE

This unusual five-piece set of belt-fittings was found in 1967 during the excavation of one of the Anglo-Saxon cemeteries at Mucking, Essex, by Mrs M. U. Jones. The body was represented only by the stains which it left in the soil, but the fittings were in their proper position at the waist, the buckle and counter-plate worn at the front, and two triangular and one rectangular mount at the back of the body. So far as is known it is the only complete set of such equipment, and as Miss Vera Evison has said in a long study it supplies a connection between belt-equipment of the late Roman army and metalwork in the 'quoit-brooch' style of Anglo-Saxon England. Possibly it, and certain other pieces now recognized by Miss Evison, belonged to Germanic *foederati* with Roman connections who arrived early in the fifth century to assist the native population after the official withdrawal of Roman troops and remained as settlers.

The set is of bronze plate, well cast, chip-carved, inlaid with silver wire to emphasize certain geometric decoration, and with sheet silver covering the human faces, the animal bodies, and sections of the stamped decorative features.

This buckle is at present in the British Museum, but other antiquities from this now famous site may be seen in Thurrock Museum, Grays, Essex.

Length over-all 5·8 in. *British Museum. Early fifth century.*

Plate 28

SUTTON HOO: DETAIL OF PURSE-LID

The solid gold frame of the richly adorned purse-lid with its hinge-plates by which it was attached to the belt and the sliding catch by which it was opened are still in perfect condition. The substance of the purse-bag and the lid itself, perhaps of bone or ivory, have perished without trace.

The edge of the frame is inlaid with small rectangular panels and bars of garnet and *millefiori* glass, the outline being emphasized by filigree binding. On the lid were seven

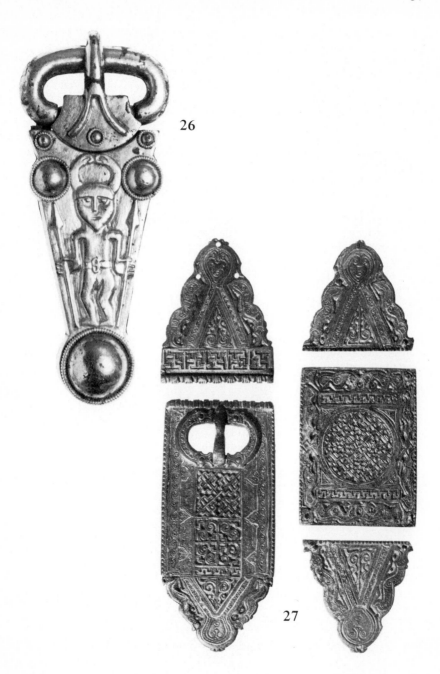

26

27

garnet-set ornamental plaques and four circular studs only one of which now retains its full setting. The plaques are in pairs except for a central double plaque, the base of which appears at the top of the enlarged photograph, which has an interlaced decoration of men and animals on a background of plain 'lidded-cloisons', a virtuosity of the jeweller's craft first recognized by Dr R. L. S. Bruce-Mitford. At first sight the garnets appear to be sunk into the surface of the gold, but this background of metal is in fact an assembly of cells which have been most carefully fitted with thick gold lids. At the top of the photograph are the lower margins of the pair of hexagonal plaques of fine intricate *cloisonné*. At the sides are small sections of the outer pair of *cloisonné* garnet-set plaques each with a man between a pair of rampant beasts, representing possibly a Frankish version of Daniel in the Den of Lions, wolves swallowing the Old Sky Father of English mythology, or more likely a Scandinavian theme derived from ultimate Eastern sources and thus a further link between Sutton Hoo and Sweden. The central plaques, emphasized in the photograph, represent two falcons stooping on their prey, a pair of ducks, remarkable for the exceptionally large garnet plates in the bodies of the birds, the minute cloisons representing tail and wing feathers and the eyes of circular garnets set with blue enamel. The whole purse-lid, as Dr Bruce-Mitford so well says,' is the most attractive and sumptuous piece of decoration ever found in a Teutonic grave.

The purse contained an heirloom or regal treasure of thirty-seven Merovingian Frankish gold coins, no two of which come from the same mint, three blanks and two ingots. Modern research suggests that they were assembled between 625 and 630. This was clearly not a merchant's hoard, and Dr Philip Grierson has made a further interesting suggestion that it represents a free man's *wergild* or blood-price which was paid to the oarsman and steersman who brought the ship to its final home. For the impressive details of this suggestion the reader is referred to Dr Grierson's paper, 'The purpose of the Sutton Hoo coins', *Antiquity*, **44** (1970), 14.

Length 7·5 in. *British Museum.*
First half of the seventh century.

Plate 29

SWORD FITTINGS

The sword-fittings recovered from the earlier excavation and illustrated here are the gold pommel of 'cocked-hat' form with its curved surfaces most skilfully set all over with garnets and details in filigree, the guard-plates, two clips of gold filigree work from the grip, two circular bosses from the scabbard, and a pair of pyramid-shaped mounts from the sword-knot.

Features of special interest in this group include the scabbard-bosses ornamented with a foliage or petal pattern and a central cross with wedge-shaped garnets and wedge-shaped covered cells. Two rows of very small carved garnets decorate the margins. These scabbard-bosses are so far unique in Britain, though

28

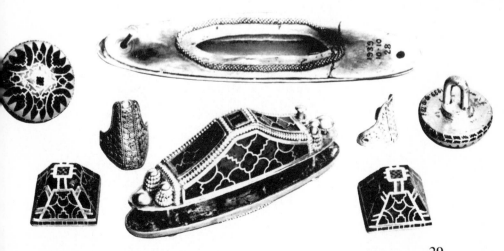

29

they appear as part of the equipment of the swords of warriors depicted on helmets found in the Vendel graves of Sweden.

The pyramid mounts have upper edges and prism-cut corners of solid garnet and the heads enclose small squares of blue glass and *millefiori* enamel of the most delicate workmanship. They bear slots at the back for attachment to the sword-knot. One can but repeat Sir Thomas Kendrick's words shortly after the discovery, that 'it can be doubted if any ancient lapidiary in the whole of the Teutonic world has produced jewels that rival these tiny pieces in the delicacy of the stone-cutting and in the accurate elegance of the assembled whole'.

Length of guard-plate 3·3 in. *British Museum.*

First half of the seventh century.

Plate 30

DETAIL OF SHOULDER-CLASP

The size, the particular curved shape, the ten strong staples on the smooth underside of each piece, and the central hinges secured by removable but attached pins all suggest that this pair of clasps was fitted to the shoulders of a thick cloth or leather cuirass. The fashion is known in some suits of Roman parade armour. The securing link-pins are attached by finely wrought gold chains and the heads are finished with animal masks decorated with small rings of filigree in which stones, probably garnets, or glass once appeared.

The main unit of design is a carpet-like spread of a central panel of fifteen step-pattern cloisons set with garnets and coloured *millefiori* glass. This has a wide surrounding border of interlaced animal pattern in garnet and, most unusually, skilfully made gold-covered cloisons which appear, visually, to be part of the background. At the outer ends of each clasp is a rounded panel decorated with intersecting pairs of tusked and crested boars most cleverly arranged with their heads in the centre and their hindquarters outstanding. The animals are decorated with most unusually large and most superbly worked plates of foil-backed garnet which are set off against a ground of fine animal and ribbon ornament in filigree.

These unique pieces are superb examples of the art and skill of the Sutton Hoo jeweller's workshop. The all-over spread of design is a portent of the later Northumbrian illuminated manuscripts, and the even later illuminations of the Lindisfarne Gospels and the Book of Kells. The boar is well-known in Celtic art, as for example on the Witham shield, and in a Christian Saxon context as decoration on an eleventh-century tympanum at Ipswich, but here it joins the Bifrons buckle from Kent and the handle of a pot-lid from Stade near Hamburg as a rare example of its use in pagan Saxondom. Here naturalistic and abstract art both find place.

Length 4·9 in. *British Museum.*

First half of the seventh century.

Plate 31

THE GREAT GOLD BUCKLE

This massive buckle, probably the fastening or decoration of the hip-to-shoulder belt which carried the sword, was found near the sword with other jewelled mountings, but closer to the remains of the purse

31

30

which was also carried on a waist-belt, all in relative positions dictated by the decay and collapse of the wooden chamber. As bullion it is said to be the most valuable gold object ever found in Britain.

The all-over decoration of intricate ribbon-style animal and asymetrical interlace is brilliantly finished by chasing, and niello most skilfully inlaid provides a fine contrast in tone to the pale yellow of the burnished gold. The rivet bosses of plain burnished gold hold slides by which the hinged back-plate is fastened.

In specialist language the decoration would be described as an example of Style II interlaced animal ornament. The ribbon-style ornament here belongs to an Anglian repertory of design, but in it there have been recognized influences from the Vendel culture of the Swedish boat-graves, and possibly even from Italy and Roman-Germanic jewellers. Some resemblance to certain illuminated initial letters in the Lindisfarne Gospels and to the art of Pictish stone-carving has also been suggested. There seems no doubt that it came from an English workshop, though it differs much from the fine polychrome jewellery of both Kent and Sutton Hoo itself.

Length 5·2 in. Weight 14·62 oz. *British Museum.*

First half of the seventh century.

Plate 32

THE ALFRED JEWEL

The discovery of the pear-shaped Alfred Jewel, a valued treasure of the University of Oxford, has already been mentioned. From the early days of its discovery the Saxon inscription cut in openwork around its edge, + AELFRED MEC HEHT GEWYRCAN, was correctly read as *'Alfred ordered me to be made'* and thought to refer to King Alfred (871–901). There can be no absolute certainty but the inscription, together with the evidence of the *cloisonné* enamel and the decoration which suggest that the jewel was made late in the ninth century, and the significance of its find-spot near the Isle of Athelney from where Alfred attacked the Viking invaders in 878 and later founded a monastery all point in the one way, so that it is not difficult to believe that this masterpiece is associated with the first King of the English.

It depicts a half-length male figure apparently seated on a stool and bearing in each hand a stem with floral head. His garment is of transparent green enamel set off with brown facings; he has grey eyes and hair and ivory-coloured flesh set against a background of transparent dark blue, all being set on a gold plate and covered by a bevelled plate of rock crystal. The unusual shape of the crystal may have determined that of the jewel. The wide terminal socket which houses a gold pin to secure a shaft of wood or perhaps ivory which has perished is fashioned in the very English-looking form of an animal head with gaping eyes and enriched with granulated work. The reverse of the gold case, as may be seen in its present skilful mounting in the Ashmolean Museum, is traced with an elaborate foliage and scale decoration, Carolingian as well as English in its inspiration.

But what was the nature and use of this fascinating jewel? It has been variously described as an amulet, a

32

32

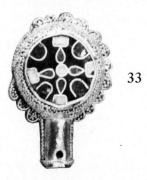

33

pendant, the head of a stylus, the head of a Roman-style battle staff, the head of a manuscript roller, the head of a small sceptre of which the Minster Lovell jewel was the foot terminal, and the central jewel of a crown of which Minster Lovell was a part. It may well have been an *aestel* or pointer used for indicating the lines in a manuscript to a reader or copyist, and here there is a literary association with King Alfred's proposed gift of his translation of Pope Gregory's *Pastoral Care* with an accompanying *aestel* to each of the English bishoprics. The figure has been described at various times as Christ, the Pope, the King himself, or one of his favourite saints, but if it is indeed a symbolic representation of Sight as Dr Egil Bakka has suggested (*Antiquaries Journal*, **46** [1966], 277–82) in a comparison with the symbolic representation of Sight on the Fuller brooch, then the probability of use as an *aestel* or pointer becomes much more likely. Further, the eyes of the figure are inclined sideways to the right and this would exclude representations of Christ, the Pope, Alfred himself, or a Saint, all of whom would have had forward looking or possibly the downcast Eyes of Majesty. It is in any case an outstanding piece of ninth-century craftsmanship, possibly by a Winchester or Glastonbury jeweller, or by a European attached to the royal court.

Length 2·45 in. Thickness 0·5 in.
Ashmolean Museum, Oxford.
Late ninth century.

Plate 33

THE MINSTER LOVELL JEWEL

This small but fine piece of late Saxon *cloisonné* enamel in the Ashmolean Museum is as well-known to specialists as its renowned neighbour, the Alfred Jewel, with which it has a similarity of form, technique, and perhaps also of purpose. It was found *c.* 1860 in circumstances not recorded at Minster Lovell near Witney, Oxfordshire, and from an Oxford jeweller passed into the hands of the Revd John Wilson, FSA, President of Trinity College, who not long after its discovery presented the jewel to the Ashmolean.

It is essentially a gold mounting for a stave or pointer, the socket for which with its cross-rivet still remains. The central feature, encased in a bent wire and granulated setting, is a roundel of *cloisonné* enamel on gold, the design on a dark blue enamel ground being a four-pointed green star with a white centre and a rectangular cell of white enamel at each tip, and between the stars of four hoop-shaped cells with light blue enamel. The surface is flat and the walls thick, as in the Alfred Jewel. The back of the jewel is flat and quite plain; the outline is emphasized by a frill of granulated decoration, and there is no doubt that this little object was meant to be seen from the front. It could have been the head of a small pointer. There seems no doubt that it was made in Britain, and it has been suggested that it could have been the foot of a sceptre or pointer topped by the Alfred Jewel, particularly if as seems likely the latter was the purpose of the larger jewel, though it has also been suggested that on stylistic grounds the Minster Lovell jewel may be a little later in date than the Alfred Jewel.

Length 1·25 in. Thickness 0·4 in.
Ashmolean Museum, Oxford.
Late ninth century.

Index